THE TOTAL FLAMENCO GUITARIST

>> A Fun and Comprehensive Overview of Flamenco Guitar Playing

JONATHAN "JUANITO" PASCUAL

Alfred Music
P.O. Box 10003
Van Nuys, CA 91410-0003
alfred.com

ISBN-10: 0-7390-4350-1 (Book & CD)
ISBN-13: 978-0-7390-4350-9 (Book & CD)

Music performed by Jonathan "Juanito" Pascual on a cypress and spruce flamenco guitar made by Aaron Green
CD recorded by Collin Tilton at Bar None Studio, Northford, CT
Doug Munro (guitar), Michael Goetz (bass), Tony Garcia (percussion)

Cover Photo: © Denkou Images / Alamy
Presentation Series flamenco guitar by Aaron Green, luthier / Courtesy of Aaron Green
www.AaronGreenGuitars.com
Interior photography by Nicole Acevedo

Contents

0

Track
1

A compact disc is available with this book. Using the disc will help make learning more enjoyable and the information more meaningful. Listening to the CD will help you correctly interpret the rhythms and feel of each example. The symbol to the left appears next to each song or example that is performed on the CD. Example numbers are above the symbol. The track number below each symbol corresponds directly to the song or example you want to hear. Track 1 will help you tune to this CD.

About the Author

Jonathan "Juanito" Pascual is an American-born flamenco guitarist, composer, and teacher who draws on an extensive background as a flamenco accompanist and soloist, as well as experiences in the worlds of jazz and classical music. He began his flamenco studies in 1988 and has gone on to perform with top flamenco singers, dancers, and guitarists from Spain and the United States. Pascual has toured Europe, North America, and South America. In addition to years of study in Spain with numerous outstanding teachers—including Adam del Monte, El Parrilla de Jerez, Manolo Sanlúcar, and El Entri—Pascual holds a bachelor of music degree in contemporary improvisation from Boston's New England Conservatory of Music, where he graduated with honors in 1997.

Pascual's love of teaching began in 1991, and since then, he has gone on to share the beauty and enjoyment of flamenco as a private teacher—and in workshops and seminars—to professional and non-professional students alike, ranging in ages from 3 to 70. Since 2005, he has been the director of the annual summer immersion program "Unlocking the Art of Flamenco" at Boston's New England Conservatory.

Pascual's innovative approach to teaching flamenco music and guitar technique is based on years of working with non-Spanish students and, in part, from overcoming a debilitating, playing-related hand problem starting in the early 1990s. Pascual combines his deep love for the guitar and flamenco music with the discoveries and insights gained from years of study with master teachers, troubleshooting his own technical dilemmas, and analyzing the characteristic difficulties of the non-Spanish flamenco student.

Pascual has recorded two full-length CDs of original flamenco guitar music and has collaborated on numerous other recording projects. In addition to an active performance schedule, his music has been heard on television and radio, and in several short films.

For more about the author and his music, please visit:

www.juanitopascual.com

PHOTO BY ERIC ANTONIOU

Acknowledgements

First I'd like to thank my editor Burgess Speed and the whole crew at Alfred Music for giving me the opportunity to share my love of flamenco teaching! As an author, I am offering my own take on information and insights gleaned from so many along the way. I must give special thanks to Dima Goryachev and Catherine Larget-Caplan, who have both played a special and complementary role in my professional development, and, in turn, many of the insights in this book. I couldn't have done this without you both so generously sharing your wisdom with me.

Many thanks to all of the incredible flamenco teachers I've had (and continue to have), including Mateo Davies, Adam del Monte, Juan del Gastor, Manuel Parrilla, Dino del Monte, David Serva, El Entri, David Leisner, Pedro Cortes, Chuscales, Eliot Fisk, and Gene Bertoncini, and to the many others who have shared their knowledge and love of flamenco. Many thanks to Nicole Acevedo for the fantastic photos, and special thanks to my students for your enthusiasm, devotion, and the learning that comes from teaching you.

Introduction

Welcome to *The Total Flamenco Guitarist!* It is sincerely hoped that this book will serve as a useful and inspiring guide to help you discover your passion and fulfill your potential on the flamenco guitar.

Origins of Flamenco

Flamenco music and culture originated in the southernmost part of the Iberian Peninsula, the region in Spain known as Andalucia. This geographically isolated spot (mountains to the north, ocean to the south and west) has been home to a unique melting pot of cultures over many centuries, with the art of flamenco being among the region's most distinct legacies.

A large and diverse group of song forms, flamenco was popularized in the mid-1800s, at which time, dance and guitar accompaniment became standard parts of the genre. The music spread to other areas in Spain, most notably to Madrid and Barcelona, though the birthplace and heart of flamenco is understood to be the triangle created by the Andalucian cities of Sevilla, Cádiz, and Jerez de la Frontera.

Flamenco is a folk tradition that has achieved an extraordinary degree of refinement in its three major expressions (singing, dancing, and guitar). It is constantly evolving and has been greatly influenced by Latin American music and, in recent decades, by jazz and many other non-Spanish styles. For many, however, flamenco represents the songs and dances they grew up with—the familiar music they sing and play at special events, including weddings, baptisms, birthdays, and holidays. For many, flamenco is regarded as a way of life.

About This Book

The five primary objectives of this book are:

1. To provide a general orientation and act as a resource to guide your exploration of flamenco music and culture

2. To give a progressive method to develop the major techniques used in flamenco

3. To establish a progressive method to learn the four primary rhythms used in flamenco

4. To provide graded guitar pieces that serve as solo repertoire while building a foundation for growth beyond this book

5. To offer lots of useful tips to get the best results and make learning and playing flamenco as smooth and rewarding as possible

The Principle Behind This Method

The driving principle behind the method section of this book is simple: more with less. In other words, in this book, the truly essential technical and rhythmic ingredients of flamenco have been identified, then laid out in a step-by-step way, specifically geared to facilitate their mastery. The development of these skills makes it possible to not only learn and master the material in the repertoire section (later in the book), but is also intended to serve as the core of a solid, potentially lifelong practice to which you may add on and customize as you learn and incorporate new material.

Who Is This Book For?

This book is for anyone curious about flamenco. If you've simply heard flamenco and want to know how some of those sounds and rhythms are played, or you are starting on a path as a professional performer or passionate aficionado, there is something here for you. This book can help you absorb specific things you might be curious about or can, indeed, if gone through systematically, provide a foundation to help guide you as far as you aspire to go.

How to Use This Book

Listen, listen, listen... There is no single way to learn, or use a book, but following are some strong suggestions on how to get the most from this book.

1. Before playing a given selection yourself, listen to it many times on the accompanying CD. When learning the repertoire selections, it would be ideal to be able to sing a piece from memory before beginning to learn it.

2. If you're learning with a teacher, have him/her teach what you have been listening to—by playing for you, and you repeating until memorized, rather than learning it first from the written page.

3. Only after following steps 1 and 2 above should you begin using the notated music. Let the written page serve as more of a reminder of what was already shown to you, as opposed to being the main source for how the piece is supposed to be played. In either case, the clearer you have the sound of this music in your mind, the easier it is to get that sound in your own playing.

About the Music in This Book

All of the musical selections, both the shorter examples and full pieces, were composed specifically for this book. The feel of these pieces is decidedly traditional, and they are all meant to be:

1. Enjoyable to play and listen to, yet approachable by people who may be relatively new to flamenco

2. Representative of a solid, traditional flamenco vocabulary, from which one can then build upon—an essential reference as you evolve as a player

3. Performable as solo pieces but also sources for smaller segments that may be picked out and mixed with material learned elsewhere in the same rhythms

A Few More Thoughts

Creating this all-in-one flamenco guitar method has been an exciting and challenging process. Flamenco guitar has and continues to be an oral, or "aural," tradition, with material passed on from teacher to student or colleague to colleague, face to face, note by note, until passages are committed to memory. In recent decades, this tradition has been expanded by guitarists' extensive use of transcribing by ear, note by note, from recordings as well. This is a great tool, and it's easier than ever with the use of software programs that slow down music without changing the pitch.

The teaching of flamenco through a method book, like transmission of any style of music by written means alone, can never fully convey certain elements of the art form. Elements such as subtlety of tone, the feeling of a strong internalized rhythm, phrasing, or simply the feeling of being in a room full of people communicating in this exhilarating "language" cannot be conveyed by a book. And so, you should seek out live flamenco whenever possible.

Today, the internet provides unprecedented access to endless videos of the great artists of the genre, as well as providing a view of flamenco in less formal settings. Watch and enjoy as much flamenco as possible. The list of artists in the appendix of this book (pages 121–126), and the rhythms covered throughout, provide a great place to start your journey.

This book is not meant to substitute the important elements absorbed through live experience or to take the place of a patient and capable teacher. It is hoped, however, that this book will offer not only a useful explanation of all the fundamental techniques, major rhythms, and enjoyable solo pieces, but that the musical and cultural fundamentals of this deep and fascinating art are touched on in a way that provides a sound foundation and direction for further discovery.

Consistent practice and lots of listening are two vital keys to learning flamenco. We hope this book will inspire your curiosity and diligence, and that you will find it a rewarding musical journey!

Chapter 1: Getting Started

In this chapter, we will look at the fundamentals, including a review of basic notation, information about the guitar, fingernails, posture and technique, and a basic approach to learning flamenco.

Basic Notation Review

Reading Tablature (TAB)

Tablature, or TAB, is a system used for guitar and other fretted instruments. There are six lines that represent the strings. Numbers are placed on the lines; these numbers tell you what frets to play. The top line represents the 1st string and the bottom line represents the 6th string. In this book, TAB is written below the corresponding standard music notation.

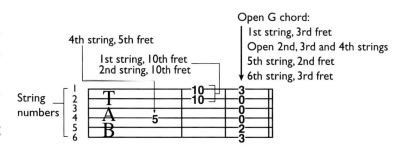

Chord Diagrams

Chord diagrams illustrate how chords are to be formed on the fretboard. Vertical lines represent strings, and horizontal lines represent frets.

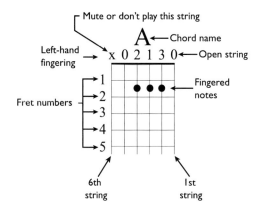

Standard Music Notation

Notes

Music is written by placing *notes* on a *staff.* Notes appear in various ways.

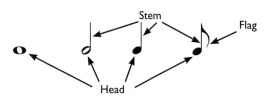

The Staff and Clef

The staff has five lines and four spaces, which are read from left to right. At the beginning of the staff is a *clef.* The clef dictates what notes correspond to a particular line or space on the staff. Guitar music is written in *treble clef* 𝄞, which is sometimes called the *G clef.* The ending curl of the clef circles the G line on the staff.

Below are the notes on the staff using the G clef.

Notes on the Lines   Notes in the Spaces

E   G   B   D   F   D   F   A   C   E   G

Ledger Lines

The higher a note appears on the staff, the higher it sounds.
When a note is too high or too low to be written on the
staff, *ledger lines* are used.

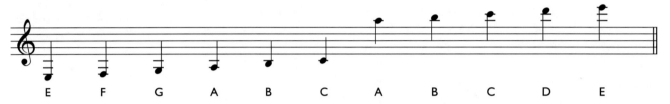

E   F   G   A   B   C   A   B   C   D   E

Musical Time, Measures, and Barlines

Musical time is measured in *beats*. Beats are the steady
pulse of the music on which we build *rhythms*. Rhythm
is a pattern of long and short sounds and silences and
is represented by *note* and *rest values*. Value indicates
duration.

The staff is divided by vertical lines called *barlines*. The
space between two barlines is a *measure*, or *bar*. Measures
divide music into groups of beats. A *double barline* marks
the end of a section or example.

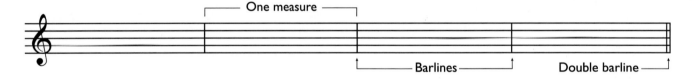

Note Values

The duration of a note—its value—is indicated by the note's appearance or shape.

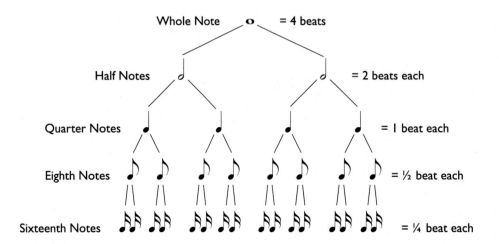

Time Signatures

A *time signature* appears at the beginning of a piece of music. The number on top indicates the number of beats per measure. The number on the bottom indicates the type of note that gets one beat.

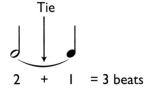

$\frac{4}{4}$ = 4 beats per measure
Quarter note ♩ = one beat

$\frac{3}{4}$ = 3 beats per measure
Quarter note ♩ = one beat

$\frac{6}{8}$ = 6 beats per measure
Eighth note ♪ = one beat

Sometimes a **C** is used in place of $\frac{4}{4}$.
This is called *common time.*

Ties and Counting

A *tie* is a curved line that joins two or more notes of the same pitch that last the duration of the combined note values. For example, when a half note (two beats) is tied to a quarter note (one beat), the combined notes are held for three beats (2 + 1 = 3).

Notice the numbers under the staff in the examples to the right. These indicate how to count while playing. Both of these examples are in $\frac{4}{4}$ time, so we count four beats in each measure. *Eighth-note* rhythms are counted "1–&, 2–&, 3–&," etc. The numbers are the *onbeats* and the "&"s (pronounced "and") are the *offbeats*.

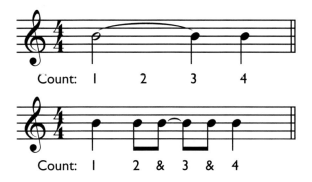

Tie

2 + 1 = 3 beats

Count: 1   2   3   4

Count: 1   2 & 3 & 4

Triplets

A *triplet* is a group of three notes that divides a beat (or part of a beat) into three equal parts.

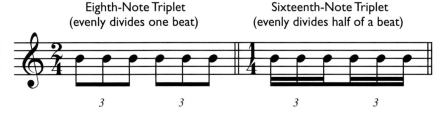

Eighth-Note Triplet
(evenly divides one beat)

Sixteenth-Note Triplet
(evenly divides half of a beat)

3   3   3   3

Dots

A *dot* increases the length of a note or rest by one half of its original value. For instance, a half note lasts for two beats. Half of its value is one beat (a quarter note). So a *dotted half note* equals three beats (2 + 1 = 3), which is the same as a half note tied to a quarter note. The same logic applies for all dotted notes.

Dotted notes are especially important when the time signature is $\frac{3}{4}$, because the longest note value that will fit in a measure is a dotted half note. Also, dotted notes are very important in $\frac{6}{8}$ time, because not only is a dotted half note the longest possible note value, but a dotted quarter note is exactly half of a measure (counted: 1–&–ah, 2–&–ah).

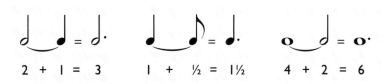

2 + 1 = 3   1 + ½ = 1½   4 + 2 = 6

2 + 1 = 3   1 + ½ = 1½   4 + 2 = 6

Count: 1   2   3   1 & ah 2 & ah

Parts of the Guitar

Below is a picture of a guitar, with all of its parts labeled.

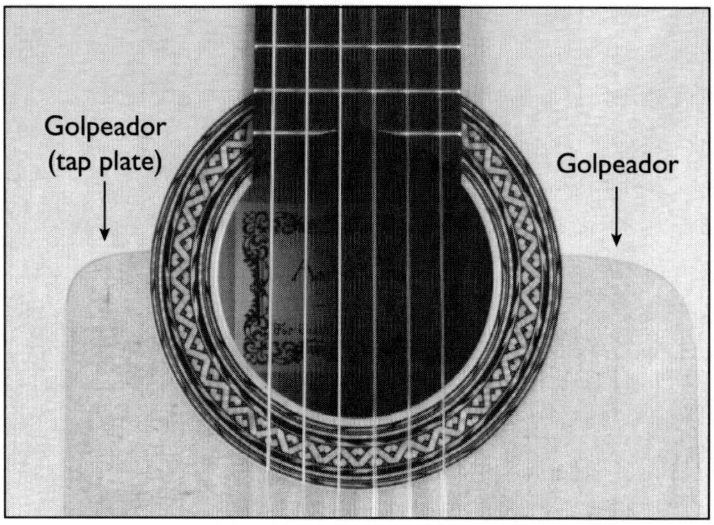

Headstock

Tuning Pegs/Machines

Nut

Neck/Fingerboard

Strings

Frets

Golpeador (tap plate)

Golpeador

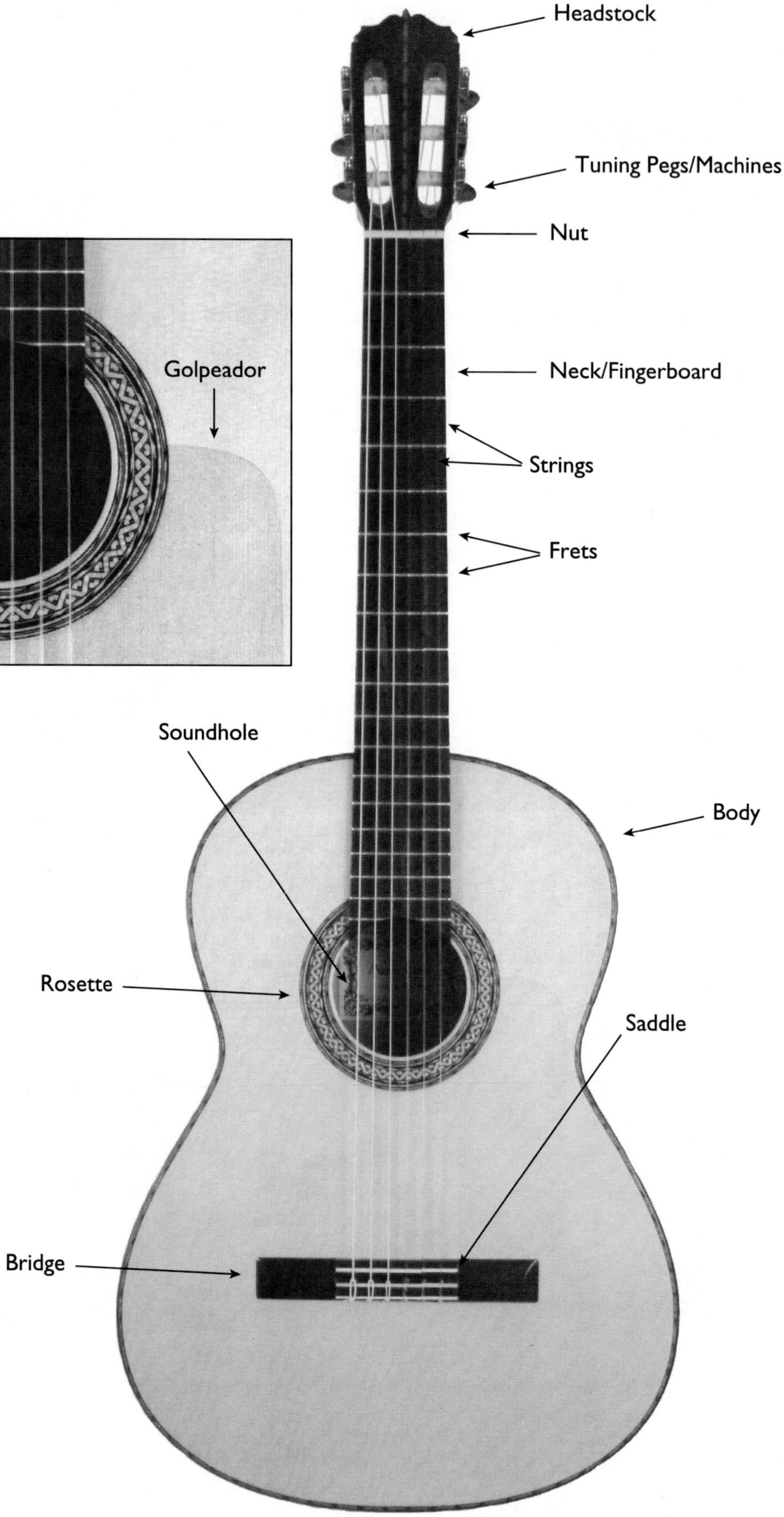

Soundhole

Body

Rosette

Saddle

Bridge

About the Instrument

The flamenco guitar has much in common with most other 6-string guitars, but with a few very important distinguishing features. It is most similar to a classical guitar in that it uses nylon strings, as opposed to the steel strings of the folk guitar. Traditionally, the woods used were cypress for the back and sides, and spruce for the top, though occasionally cedar is used instead. To this day, the cypress/spruce team is regarded as the standard for flamenco guitars. However, Brazilian or Indian rosewood on the back and sides have become popular in recent decades. The denser rosewood, often the wood of choice for the classical guitar, provides a darker tone and more sustain than the less dense and therefore more percussive response typical of cypress wood. The string height for flamenco guitars also tends to be closer to the fingerboard than a classical guitar, allowing the strings to buzz just slightly on the frets, adding an edge to the sound, which is characteristic in flamenco. Much of the time, the flamenco guitar serves as a drum, as well as a chordal and melodic instrument. It is equipped with a *golpeador,* or *tap plate,* allowing the player to strike the face of the guitar in various ways (to be looked at later in the book), without scratching or eventually wearing a hole in the guitar. Finally, another big difference is on the inside of the guitar, where the internal wooden bracing system that holds it all together is filed to be relatively thin and light; again, this is to facilitate a fast, percussive response, a sonic quality that reflects the clapping and heel work that are so integral to flamenco.

Flamenco Tuning

The *standard tuning* used in flamenco is the same as in most other styles of guitar. All of the material covered in this book will use the following tuning:

6th = Low E
5th = A
4th = D
3rd = G
2nd = B
1st = High E

The only consistent exception to this comes when playing the musical form of *rondeña* (originating from the Spanish town of Ronda in the province of Málaga), which uses a tuning where the 6th string is lowered from E to D, and the 3rd string is lowered from G to F♯.

In recent years, many guitarists have explored their own alternate tunings to create a different mood, often tuning the low E to a D, or lower, to expand the range of the instrument. It is fairly common to hear pieces on contemporary flamenco CDs where the guitarist has devised their own tuning.

How Do You Hold the Guitar?

This is an extremely important question and one that can, in some cases, take a surprisingly long time to answer.

Unlike classical guitar technique, which has its standard approach of elevating the left leg with a foot stool, flamenco is a little more varied. Demonstrated below are the most common ways to hold the guitar. The final decision, however, is up to you. Experiment. See what feels most comfortable and helps you get the most out of your instrument.

Your main concerns when choosing a position are comfort of the back, shoulders, and neck—plus complete freedom of the arms. It is extremely important that you find a position in which you could comfortably sit—without the guitar—for the same amount of time you will be spending with the guitar.

Position 1: Traditional.

Position 2: Modern.

Position 3: Elevation of right leg with foot stool (or guitar case).

Position 4: Use of leg rest (blends the good points of the traditional and modern positions).

Fingernails

While the fingernail (or just "nail") is an extremely important element in the sound of the flamenco guitar, we will begin learning the basic techniques *without* nails on the right (strumming) hand. Starting without nails gives our fingers a solid connection to the strings. Once we allow our nails to grow out a bit, we can use this sense of connection as a reference for comfort and ease of movement. Often, the nails can hook or snag on the string, so getting a good feeling for the finger with no nail will help us maintain an easy and snag-free attack.

Nails on the right hand are a fundamental part of the flamenco sound. They also play a role on the left (fretting) hand. Fretting-hand nails should be kept quite short—long enough to support the flesh at the tip of the finger, but short enough that they are not touching the fretboard.

Nail Length

Like many aspects of flamenco, the norms for nail length and shape have evolved over the years. The general trend with nails has gone from longer to shorter. Many of the great virtuoso players of today—including Paco de Lucía, Manolo Sanlúcar, and Vicente Amigo—keep their nails quite short. This approach is based on the desire to have enough nail present to brighten the tone, while having no excess nail to slow down the overall duration of each attack; in other words, shorter nails facilitate maximum speed and fluidity, while producing a desirable tone as well.

Nail Shape

Not only is nail length extremely important, but so is nail shape. For most of us, the natural shape of the unfiled nail will not be conducive to optimal sound or smooth flow on the strings.

For the flamenco guitarist, the nail is indeed a part of our instrument, in some ways akin to the bow used by violinists. Proper length and shape will have a significant effect on not only one's basic sound, but also on one's rate of progress, as poorly shaped nails can really slow things down.

What to Look for in Your Nails

Like most other aspects of guitar, finding the "perfect" nail length and shape is an ongoing process. The nail is, literally, different every day and is therefore a moving target. One day it may seem perfect and then the next day, not so; you go to file it, perhaps a bit too much, then have to wait a few days for it to grow back, and so on…

The basic concept to have in mind is that the nail should be long enough to touch the string, but not any longer. If a little more length gives stability, that is fine and worth experimenting with. Just remember that shorter nails are generally conducive to more ease of playing.

For most people, it is necessary to file down the edge of the nail where the nail and flesh meet the string. Excessive length here can cause the nail to catch, or scrape, the string. The correct nail curve and length are shown in the picture below.

Some people's nails are wavy and curve downward. If this is the case for you, it is important to pay extra attention to filing your nail upward to gradually redirect the nail growth. If your nails hook downward, it may be best to cut them off entirely, as hooking nails will significantly slow development.

If your nails do hook down, you can address this partly in the following way.

1. Soak them so they become softer.

2. Dry them off.

3. Apply some nail hardener, or nail glue, to the nail while flattening the tip at the edge of a table or other flat surface (see photo below).

4. Allow the nail hardener to dry with the nail in the new, flatter position.

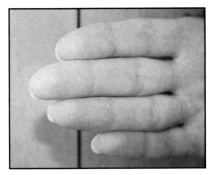

Correct nail curve and length.

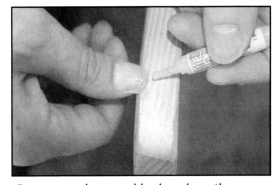

Correcting a downward hook to the nails.

The Role of the Nail

The nail is used in guitar playing to give a brightness and clarity that is not there when we pluck with only the skin; it also gives volume and helps project the sound outward from the body of the instrument. This projection of sound is a key element in all of the major right-hand flamenco techniques.

A well-shaped nail will flow easily over the string, but needs to be long enough to make contact and brighten the note. When nails are just right, there is a feeling of support and leverage that helps project the note in a way that seems disproportionate to the amount of energy being put into it—like a natural amplifier.

Time, experimentation, and daily vigilance are important factors in getting your nails just right. It is necessary to have a variety of nail files and/or grades of sandpaper (from medium grade to extremely fine) on hand for the daily care of your nails. It is actually a big time-saver, in the long run, to make sure at the beginning of each practice session that your nails are smooth and not catching on the strings. Sometimes, the temptation to just start playing leads us to ignore roughness in the nail that, in turn, leads to poor sound and erratic technique—not a good use of our valuable time.

Strengthening the Nail

Many people find that the techniques of flamenco playing tear up their nails. However, as one's technique evolves—becoming more and more relaxed—the nails act more as a bridge allowing a transfer of weight from the hand into the string, with impact on the nails being less and less. That being said, everyone's nails are different, and if you wind up playing with dancers, singers, and other instrumentalists, the intensity of playing is likely to take a toll. Because of this, you should consider some of the following ways to strengthen your nails.

Many people use products, including drugstore nail hardeners and, very commonly, nail glue. Often, a single layer or two of nail glue on the last third of the nail is sufficient to keep it from breaking. If glue alone is not doing the trick, silk wraps and/or acrylic powder can be added to the glue, then carefully shaped and buffed, creating extremely hard nails.

Do not get salon acrylic nails. These tend to be clunky and lead to very poor sound. Also, for the sake of overall nail health, it is recommended, when using nail glues, to cover the least amount of nail possible while still doing the job. These products tend to damage the nail slightly when they come off, causing a weakening in the nail, and in turn creating more dependency on the glues. There are also cases of guitarists developing destructive nail funguses from prolonged use of these products. So, while many professional flamenco guitarists rely on these products, use them with caution, and avoid them if possible.

Today, there are various "fake nail" products that have been created specifically for guitarists and intended to not damage the nail underneath. You may want to explore these options if you find your own nail simply will not stop breaking or tearing.

Diet is also a factor in nail health, and further research into the effects of certain types of food may yield helpful information.

Important Filing Tips

1. Always file in one direction only, as opposed to a back and forth. A back and forth movement disturbs the grain of the nail and makes it more susceptible to breaking.

2. While filing, gently press upward with your file to direct the nail a bit upward, like the tip of a ski. While a downward hook can catch on the string, a slight upward tendency can really help the nail glide right over the string.

3. Finish the process by rubbing the nail tip on your jeans, a piece of leather, or a very fine grade of sandpaper. This, again, helps the nail achieve optimal smoothness.

4. Try glass nail files. These have become quite popular and offer a great deal of control that is well worth the extra cost.

What Is a "Total Flamenco Guitarist?"

Being a total, or well-rounded, flamenco guitarist is actually a bit different than some may think, especially if their primary contact with flamenco has been hearing or seeing solo guitar performances. The history and evolution of the flamenco guitar is that of a humble accompaniment to singers and dancers. The significance of this point cannot be overstated. Without exception, all of the legendary concert flamenco guitarists are also among the greatest accompanists in the tradition, from early masters Ramón Montoya and Niño Ricardo to more modern masters Sabicas, Paco de Lucía, and Tomatito. The importance of rhythm, the sense of phrasing, and many more vital components in solo guitar playing all make their first appearance in this accompaniment context.

With that in mind, it is safe to say that a well-rounded flamenco guitarist, in the traditional setting, has the following:

1. Command of the rhythms of all the primary forms of flamenco, which will be addressed throughout this book

2. A substantial knowledge of the songs themselves. Even guitarists who don't consider themselves singers can hum the basic melodies—in the correct rhythmic structures—to a wide range of songs. Many guitarists are, in fact, quite good singers as well.

3. Some experience with the accompaniment of flamenco dancers. This varies greatly in Spain from person to person. Historically, for many professional guitarists, their entire career is based around dance accompaniment, while others may be primarily accompanists to singers.

4. A repertoire of solo passages, known as *falsetas*, in each of the forms. These short melodic sections are used as interludes when accompanying both singers and dancers, and form the basis of a player's solo repertoire. While many books on flamenco guitar focus on learning falsetas, this book uses a more comprehensive approach that develops the skills used in *all* facets of flamenco guitar—including, but not limited to, falsetas and solo guitar playing.

Learning Flamenco—A Three-Pronged Approach

The approach to learning flamenco presented in this section is at the very foundation of everything that follows in this book. It is an approach specifically tailored to enable a student of any background to develop his or her potential to the fullest—avoiding the pitfalls that so often accompany the learning of this multi-dimensional form of music. Indeed, this is a golden age for the non-Spanish student of flamenco, with access at an unprecedented level to recordings and videos of this previously elusive art form.

The three-pronged approach presented here is simple and yet extremely powerful in its ability to facilitate an optimal learning experience over time.

The three areas, or *prongs*, are:

1. Rhythm

Flamenco is fundamentally a rhythmic style of music. Those who grow up in a flamenco-based culture learn the songs and rhythms at an early age, well before they are even big enough to begin learning to play a guitar. It is not uncommon to see children—as young as 3, 4, and 5 years of age—singing, dancing, and clapping out the rhythms (*palmas,* see page 119) with a great deal of skill. All of these rhythms are, therefore, already a part of them when they do finally get a guitar in their hands at age 7 or 10 or 15.

2. Technique

Technique development becomes central to the practice of most developing and professional flamenco guitarists. In this book, the designation of technique as a separate prong has to do with the realization that many newcomers tend to throw themselves into playing the material—repertoire that is filled with new and unfamiliar rhythms and techniques. This tendency has led many an aspiring guitarist to play for years and yet still never be able to play freely or comfortably. The approach in this book therefore separates the three vital prongs—allowing time to develop technical comfort and rhythmic fluency—that they may naturally converge as the material progresses.

3. Listening

Listening to flamenco is the cornerstone of a truly effective flamenco learning plan. It is not uncommon for someone to hear flamenco once or twice and be really inspired to learn it. They may wind up seeking instruction while having listened to very little actual flamenco music. Again, in its native environment, the process is usually quite the opposite. By the time a person would actually begin playing guitar, they can usually sing, clap, maybe dance, and even mimic very accurately some of the strumming techniques (if they've been around enough guitarists). This internalization of the music is ultimately a major determining factor in the depth one winds up attaining in their flamenco guitar playing—and should be regarded as equally important to the time actually spent with the guitar.

To summarize this approach, we have three initially separate, but concurrent tracks of learning: rhythmic development, technical practice, and listening. Listening (to both singers and guitarists) can start immediately; there is a list of major artists in the appendix section of this book. Technique and rhythm exercises will be taught in the following pages.

By working on the three prongs separately, we can see how each element informs and enhances the other. For example, as you learn some of the specific techniques, you will begin to notice them when listening to recordings or seeing people perform. In addition, as you learn some of the rhythms, you will hear them in recordings; listening will help you internalize those rhythms more deeply, and you will be able to discern which techniques are being used to generate those rhythms on the guitar.

This separation gives an opportunity to experience clarity and develop comfort with the vital components of this style. It also helps avoid the confusion and struggle that often occurs to the student who tries to "eat the whole cake at once," hoping for the best while spending many frustrated hours with less than optimal results.

Chapter 2: The Technique Survival Kit

The "Technique Survival Kit" is based on a simple goal: to equip you with the tools needed to play real music as soon as possible, while at the same time helping you steer clear of the unnecessary struggles that can come from trying to do too many things at once. It is a distilled set of essential techniques consisting of thumb, left-hand chords, arpeggio, one type of *rasgueado* (strumming technique), and the single-note playing technique called *picado*, which is used to some degree in virtually all flamenco pieces. This kit of basic techniques will allow you to start enjoying the first pieces in this book, as well as any basic flamenco repertoire you may encounter. As we progress, we'll steadily add new techniques and variations on the basic techniques, thus expanding our technical palette as we go.

While individual musical passages may be played with any single technique, generally, even the most basic solo selections require that a variety of techniques be employed. In other words, a selection may go from thumb to arpeggio to picado back to arpeggio and so on. Indeed, this constant shifting from one technique to the next is one of the ways we are able to tell an interesting and varied story through our playing.

In this section, we'll learn the basic setup for each of the critical techniques mentioned above and a few ways to practice each one. Following the progression laid out here, you'll realize upon arriving at the musical selections later in the book that you have already prepared much of what is needed to play the pieces, making enjoyment and musicality in the repertoire selections much more immediate than it might otherwise be.

To the right is the Technique Survival Kit Checklist. It is a list of everything you'll be working on in this section in preparation for the pieces that come later in the book.

Technique Survival Kit Checklist	
√	**Thumb**
√	Strumming
√	Single-note playing
√	**Left Hand**
√	Introduction to chords
√	**First rasgueado**
√	**Picado**
√	Right hand
√	Left hand
√	**Arpeggio**

One of the most important things to realize about this kit is that, while it is paving the way to begin playing comfortably, it is also the core of a basic daily practice routine that you may use indefinitely. Many professionals use just such a condensed set of exercises to keep themselves in shape.

This approach also addresses the reality of needing to make the most of what, often, is limited practice time. This is a straightforward set of exercises that can directly improve the foundations of your playing for as long you play the guitar.

Setting Up the Thumb

The thumb and rasgueado produce the quintessential sounds of flamenco guitar. Historically, these two techniques were *the* techniques—rasgueado for accompaniment and the thumb for melody lines and additional strumming. A thumb that produces a rich, clear, and, at times, punchy tone is an essential component of flamenco guitar playing. Let's get started!

Using Weight

One of the keys to comfortable, good-sounding playing is to allow the weight of the forearm and hand to do the work for you, as opposed to tense, muscle-forced playing. Even if you're relatively thin, the weight of the bone and muscle from the elbow down is more than what's needed to activate the strings. Take a moment to loosely shake the forearm and hand so that it becomes relaxed. This "dead weight" is the source of our power when playing. The same principle is at work here as when you let the weight of a hammer do the work of pounding a nail. This principle is also apparent in sports like golf and tennis, and in the martial arts—visible in those displays of breaking boards. The key to maximum power in all these areas is the same: *allowing* rather than *doing*.

Now that you've taken a moment to free up your arm, place your thumb on the 6th string of your guitar and allow the weight of the forearm and hand to rest on the strings *into* the guitar, as opposed to down towards the ground. Give the weight of the forearm and hand over to the strings and allow the hand to be supported by the strings. The thumb resting on the strings is akin to resting your head on a pillow. Therefore, the hand should relax, like when you hang your thumb in your pants pocket while the fingers hang freely down. (See photos below.)

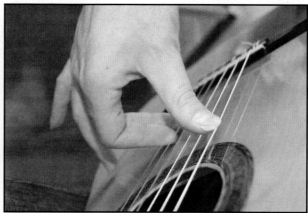

Allow the weight of your forearm and hand to do the work for you. Place your thumb on the 6th string, and allow the weight of your forearm and hand to rest on the strings into *the guitar, as opposed to down towards the ground.*

The thumb and fingers should be quite loose. You can gently shake the hand out if you feel some tension. Rolling the shoulders is also an excellent way to loosen up the entire arm, including the hand.

Next, simply "wipe" your finger off by going from the 6th string through the 1st string. The feeling here is as if you're using the strings to clean something sticky off your thumb. In other words, there is a lot of flesh in contact with the strings, pushing inward to create solid contact. All the time, the hand is loose and the weight of the arm is going into the guitar. Make sure during this process that you're not holding your breath (as this would be a source of tension), but breathing steadily.

"Wipe" your finger off by going from the 6th string through the 1st string.

Now, repeat this process. You will notice that this combination of being very loose, with the act of "wiping" something off of the thumb, results in a certain amount of sound. Keep repeating the process, and increase the volume as you do so. Try shifting the angle of the thumb and notice how the tone and volume also shift as you try different angles.

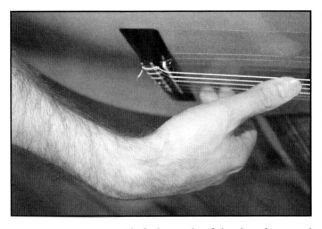

Shift the angle of the thumb to produce changes in tone and volume.

The process above is the beginning of playing flamenco! It is well known in the flamenco world that the great players will very often sit down at the beginning of their day and just "thumb through" the guitar strings, playing one or two simple chords as they warm up. This can last for 30 or 40 minutes and relates to a central theme of how they get so good in the first place: mastery of the basics. Poise and finesse are qualities often associated with good flamenco players, and it is precisely this type of relaxed repetition that gradually allows these qualities to emerge.

Introduction to Chords

In this section, we'll look at two of the most commonly used chords in flamenco: E Major (E) and A Minor (Amin). Look at the left-hand fingering for the E chord below, and form it on your guitar.

The E Chord

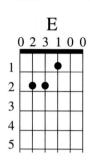

When forming chords with the left hand, keep the fingers close together. This creates a more stable structure. Additionally, having the fingertips all together creates a point, like a bird's beak, which allows the strings to sink into the fretboard more easily, thus reducing the energy or effort needed to make the chord.

The left-hand thumb should be low on the neck, and it should gently squeeze toward the fingers.

Left-hand thumb position.

Be mindful not to squeeze too hard at first, trusting that with repetition, the hand will get stronger and the fingers will start to memorize the position.

Now, strum through the E chord 16 times with your thumb, listening to the sound and making sure all six notes are clear. (Note that the left-hand finger numbers are indicated next to the notes. The fingers of the left hand are numbered 1–4 starting with the index finger.)

$\uparrow_p$ = Strum downward (from the 6th string to the 1st) with the thumb

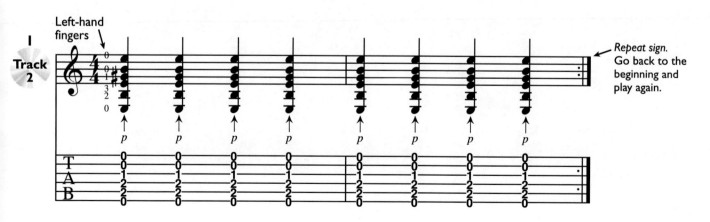

Now, check out the fingering for the A Minor chord below, and form it on your guitar.

The A Minor Chord

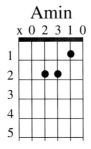

Amin
x 0 2 3 1 0

Notice the fingers are in the same configuration for the A Minor chord as they are for the E chord. Try forming the E chord, then simply shift all three fingers, together, up one string—and strum all but the low E string. Listen to this new chord.

Now, practice shifting from E to Amin, keeping the fingers together all the time and gently switching back and forth. Make sure you're breathing steadily. First, try playing four quarter notes for each chord (Example 2), then try a half note for each chord (Example 3).

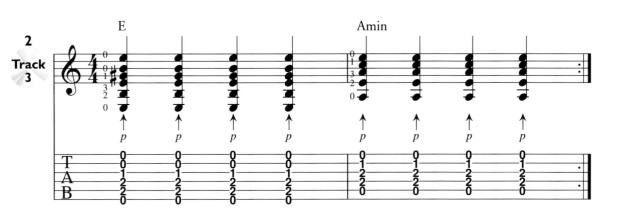

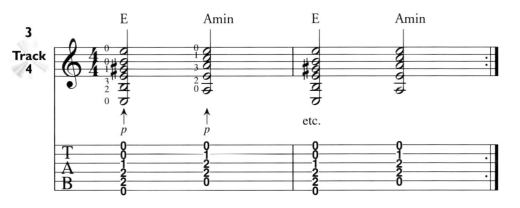

Rest Stroke and Free Stroke

The two types of right-hand strokes used to play single notes on the guitar are the *rest stroke* (*apoyando*) and *free stroke* (*tirando*). The rest stroke is a pluck where the finger lands (rests) on the string adjacent to the one just played.

The free stroke is a pluck that is followed through "in the air," in other words, *without* landing on the adjacent string.

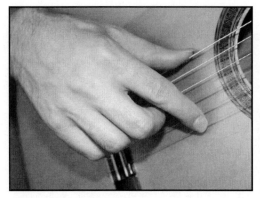

Rest-stroke set-up.

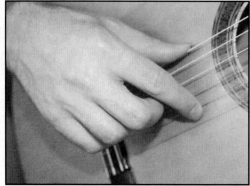

Rest-stroke follow through.

Free-stroke set-up.

Free-stroke follow through.

The differences between these two strokes have to do with volume and *timbre* (tone). The rest stroke allows a greater amount of energy to go into the string, and is generally used for louder and more emphatic passages. Flamenco makes extensive use of this technique both in the thumb and fingers. The free stroke is generally a lighter sounding technique than the rest stroke. It is often used in lyrical passages where the rest stroke might sound too choppy (*staccato*) and in techniques such as arpeggio and tremolo, which we will look at later in the book. Free stroke is the primary stroke used in much of the classical guitar repertoire and is important for flamenco as well.

Rest Stroke with Thumb

Playing single-note rest strokes with the thumb flows naturally from what we've already learned with the thumb strum. At first, the rest stroke can be approached by merely slowing down the strum so that the notes start sounding one by one.

Try the following: Starting at full speed, strum through the strings like you did on page 19. Then, over the course of 20 (or more) strums, gradually slow down enough so that you feel no change in the pressure of your right hand. In other words, don't tense up to go slower; just let the hand slow down little by little until you notice the notes sounding one by one. This is an excellent way to warm up and can be done endlessly like a meditation. This type of practice is a huge help in getting acquainted with the subtleties of tone production and can generally be very useful in gaining greater ease and comfort not only with the thumb, but with the hand overall.

Single Notes with the Thumb

Rather than a new technique, single notes with the thumb are just a further reduction of the movement discussed on the previous page. This concept is key. We've started with the large, easier movement of the strum and developed some fluency and comfort. This prepares us to do the same thing in miniature (i.e., the single note). Through extensive, relaxed repetition of the strum, the hand and arm naturally acclimate to the positions they're in and become more and more stable. This stability then facilitates the reduced movement of the single note. Feeling-wise, the single note is like a slice of the strum—the same weight and ease, just a smaller movement.

The movement of the thumb in flamenco is like a paddle. The entire thumb moves from the joint where it meets the wrist—an area called the "anatomical snuff box" because of its use as a surface from which to sniff powdered tobacco, or snuff (see Fig. 1)—and uses the large muscle in the palm called the thenar eminence (see Figs. 2 and 3). This movement needs to be effortless and independent. It can be practiced off of the guitar in your free time: riding the subway, bus, etc.

One of the most frequent problems people have is that they hit the string from underneath as they go back to play the next note. This is solved easily by using the natural rotation from the snuff box, so that after playing the note, the thumb relaxes and then rotates out a bit, swinging back up into position and avoiding an unwanted collision. (See Figs. 4–7.)

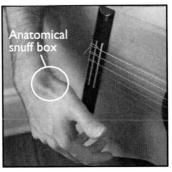

Fig. 1.

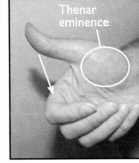

Fig. 2.

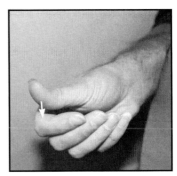

Fig. 3.

Fig. 4.

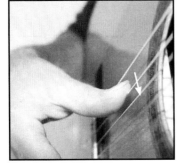

Fig. 5.

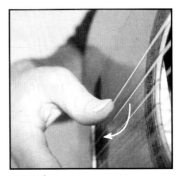

Fig. 6.

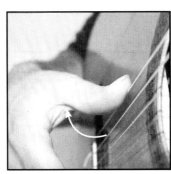

Fig. 7.

Fig. 8.

When playing single-note rest strokes with the thumb, the index and middle fingertips touch the face of the guitar while gently gripping the high-E string. The ring and middle fingers hang freely. Check out Fig. 8, then practice the following example.

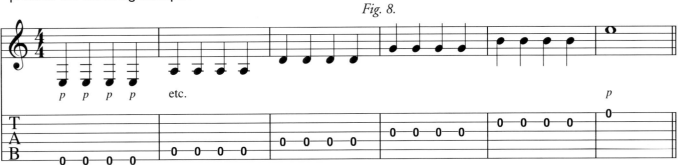

The F Chord

Before looking at the F chord below, we need to understand the term *voicing*, as it will be used in this book. There are many ways to play any given chord. A chord is defined by the notes that are in it (for example, the F Major chord is the combination of the notes F–A–C). So if we play the same notes in a different location on the neck, or on different strings, we get what are called different *voicings* of the same chord. The use of different voicings gives great variety in music and is something you'll encounter frequently when learning flamenco.

The voicing for the F chord below has a couple of extra notes—the open strings B and E. Technically, this makes it an F Major 7$^{\sharp}$11, or FMaj7$^{\sharp}$11, chord. This is a long fancy name, but the chord is easy to play, and in flamenco, it's really just thought of as another voicing for the F chord (which is how we will refer to it).

The F Chord

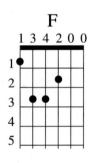

Notice the configuration of the fingers on the 5th, 4th, and 3rd strings in the diagram above. Like with the A Minor chord, this fingering is almost identical to the E chord (see diagram to the right) but up one fret and using the 2nd, 3rd, and 4th fingers. Practice making the E chord with these fingers and then sliding up one fret. Then add the 1st finger to the 1st fret of the 6th string to make the new chord.

These two chords firmly deliver the quintessential sound of flamenco guitar.

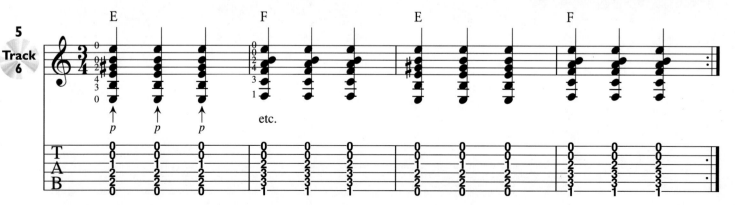

Picado

Picado is the technique used to play passages of successive single notes, like melody lines and scale runs. It is accomplished by the constant alternation of, most commonly, the index (*i*) and middle (*m*) fingers. Some players favor other combinations such as index and ring (*a*), or even a three-finger picado with ring, middle, and index (*a–m–i*). There are other combinations as well. Part of a healthy practice routine involves all of these combinations, even if you primarily only use one of them. In flamenco, the picado is nearly always played using rest strokes.

Right-Hand Fingers		
p	=	thumb
i	=	index
m	=	middle
a	=	ring
e	=	pinky

Let's take a closer look at the rest-stroke technique first covered on page 22. To play a note with rest stroke, position the hand by resting the thumb on the low-E string and the tip of the index finger on the high-E string. The note is then generated by allowing the weight of the hand—as with the thumb—to go towards the inside of the guitar and then "wiping" the tip of the finger upward across the string, allowing it to come to rest on the B string (see photos below). Now, relax and repeat

Rest-stroke set-up.

Rest-stroke follow through.

Try the rest-stroke picado exercise below, using the two-finger combinations indicated in the music. As you can see, you will be using all four of your right-hand fingers. While using the pinky (*e*) to pluck notes in flamenco is essentially not done in actual playing situations, it is good to train all of the fingers.

6

Track 7

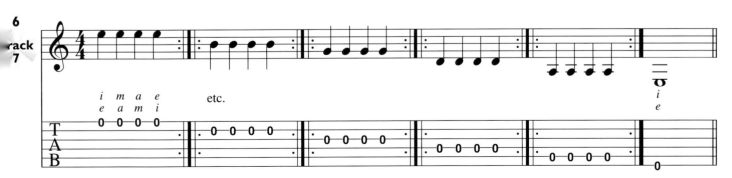

Alternation

As mentioned on the previous page, picado passages are also played by alternating the *i* and *m* fingers. In the example below, watch your right hand closely to ensure you're constantly alternating the fingers: *i-m-i-m-i-m,* etc. Development of constant alternation is a must, as it is a key to even, rhythmically solid playing.

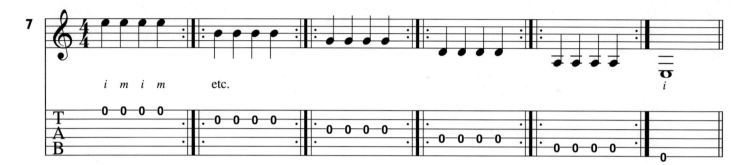

Left Hand

In the next exercise, we add the left hand. Notes are fretted with the sides of the fingertips and, like with chords, we gently squeeze the fingertips and thumb simultaneously. (See pictures below.)

Notes are fretted with the sides of the fingertips.

Correct thumb position for fretting notes.

Play the following exercise on all six strings.

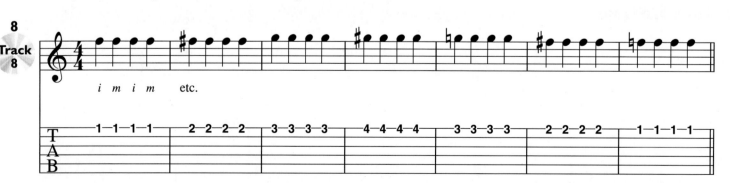

Now, let's try a scale. The scale below is known as the *Phrygian mode* and is one of the most common scales used in flamenco. For the purposes of this book, we do not need to go into the theory behind this scale; suffice it to say it is made up of all the *natural notes* (no sharps or flats) starting with the note E. So, the notes in the E Phrygian mode are E–F–G–A–B–C–D.

In the example below, we are descending from G to E and then ascending back to G. This is a good way to acquaint yourself with the scale.

E Phrygian Mode

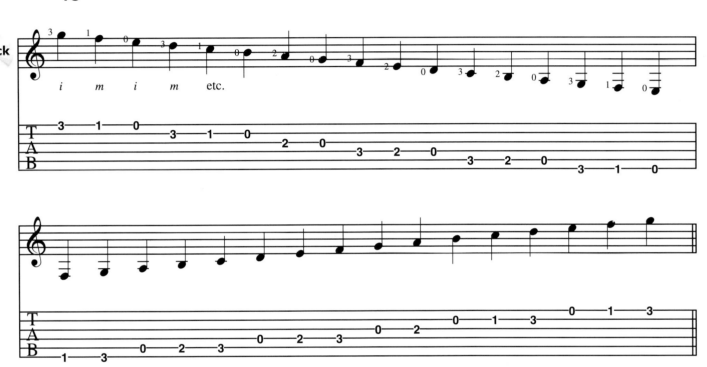

Scale Practice

The practice of scales is one of the most useful and time-tested skill builders for any instrument. Properly practiced, they are used to develop tone, coordination of the two hands, strength, and gradually, greater and greater speed and fluency throughout the instrument. The use of picado for playing fast scale runs is without a doubt one of the hallmarks of the modern era of flamenco guitar playing. However, speed in and of itself can be quite monotonous, and a single-minded quest for "burning scales" is a trap that many guitarists fall into. Super-fast scales are not a prerequisite for being a competent and expressive guitarist, and should never be a higher priority than rhythmically clear, expressive playing. In flamenco,

it is essential to "say something" with your playing—to deliver a clear emotional message, and not to get caught up in sheer physical display. As always, it is a balance; you must develop these technical tools to higher and higher levels of proficiency, while remaining connected to the emotional and spiritual core of the music.

You can practice scales either with or without a *metronome* (an adjustable time-keeping device). When working with the metronome, concentrate on your timing and speed. When working without a metronome, focus on comfort and tone.

Rasgueado

As mentioned on page 18, rasgueado, also known as *rasgueo* (pronounced ra-HEY-o), perhaps more than any other technique, really embodies the sound of flamenco. Both terms, rasgueado and rasgueo, are forms of the Spanish verb *rasguear,* meaning "to strum."

As the name implies, rasgueado is a strumming technique. There are many variations using different combinations of right-hand fingers to strum, but let's start with a good all-purpose variation, a four-finger rasgueado: *e-a-m-i.*

The following exercise is great for developing independent movement of the fingers while keeping the whole hand relaxed. (See corresponding photos to the right.)

Rasgueado Exercise

Step 1. Place the thumb on the low-E string, and let the other four fingers dangle freely.

Step 2. Place the tip joint of the pinky against the 5th and 4th strings.

Step 3. Brush through the strings as though you're using them to clean something off of the pinky.

Step 4. Repeat steps 2 and 3 with the remaining fingers one by one: *a, m,* and *i.*

Repeat the exercise above slowly for a couple of minutes, making sure you relax the hand between each stroke. The sound generated by doing this will be greatly affected by the length of the fingernails. If there is no fingernail length, the sound will be dull, as the string is likely to hit the skin at the very tip of the strumming finger. It is only once the nail begins to grow out slightly that the clearer, characteristic tone of the rasgueado begins to emerge.

Step 1.

Step 2.

Step 3.

Step 3 (follow through).

The G Chord

Below is one of the many voicings for the G Major chord. Like the F chord on page 24, this is not, technically, a straight G Major chord; because of the open E string on top, the chord becomes G6. However, in the practical tradition of flamenco (and in this book), it is referred to as G.

The G Chord

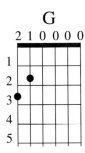

Practice the following chord sequence while strumming with the thumb.

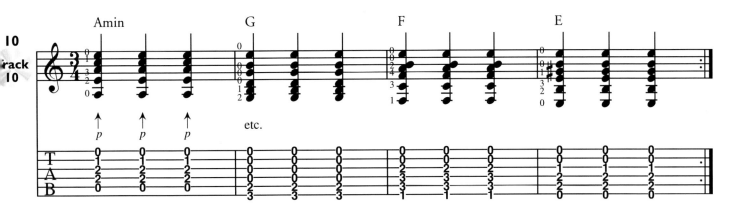

Now, try the same sequence with the rasgueado.

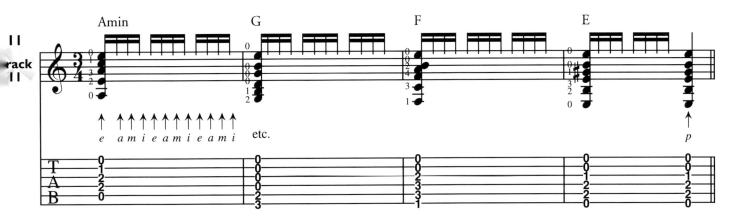

When using the rasgueado in playing, we actually bring all four fingers into a loose fist then let them drop out of the hand one by one. It is extremely important that you practice this movement away from the guitar—either in the air or on your thigh—with attention to keeping each finger loose.

Staying Loose

People often think that the rasgueado's characteristic punch and volume comes from an vigorous forcing of the fingers outward, but actually the opposite is true. In Spain, the typical player starts as a child and therefore typically has a loose, flexible hand. The joints are naturally quite supple, which, in turn, helps the fingers to be fairly independent of one another. Therefore, from the very beginning, any strength or speed emerges from that relaxed state. The most common obstacle for new students attempting to develop a comfortable, effective rasgueado is that they try to develop speed, independence, and volume all at the same time. Since as adults (and teenagers to some extent), we tend to lose some of that free movement typical of a younger hand, it becomes necessary to spend time stretching and shaking out the fingers to help them return to a more child-like state of looseness. It is particularly good to do this when the hand is quite warm, as when taking a shower or washing dishes. If you have any children under the age of 10 or 12 in your life, ask them to wiggle their hand in the air so you can see just how loose they are, and then strive to attain that looseness yourself. Age is not an issue here. Students of any age can bring great amounts of freedom into the hand through ongoing attention to stretches and develop a strong, comfortable rasgueado.

Now, practice the rasgueado from the fist. First, let all four fingers fall simultaneously. (See Figs. 1 and 2.)

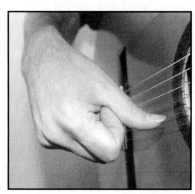
Fig. 1.

Fig. 2.

Then, do the same thing one finger at a time, retaining the same feeling of looseness felt when dropping all the fingers together. If your hand is truly loose when practicing this, the fingers should feel like they are falling out of your hand like dangling strings. If you practice this way, rather than forcing them out of the fist, the nerves and muscles—through weeks and months of relaxed practice—gradually develop power and independence without the tension that is often experienced with an approach that is too forced. (See Figs. 3–7.)

Fig. 3.

Fig. 4.

Fig. 5.

Fig. 6.

Fig. 7.

Now, try the rasgueado in tempo, while forming chords
with the left hand.

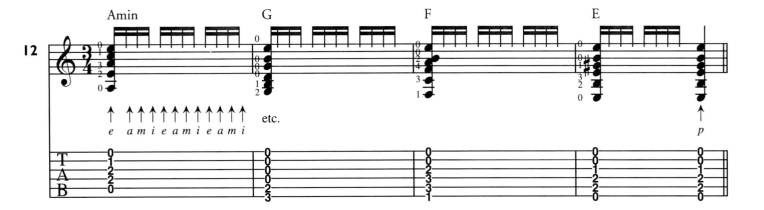

Below, we begin to practice a continuous 5-stroke
rasgueado, which adds an upstroke with the *i* finger to
what we've already practiced (see page 41 for more on this
technique). This is played as a *quintuplet,* which consists of
five notes in the time of four. In this case, five sixteenth
notes are played in the time of four sixteenth notes (in
other words, one beat).

Try this example slowly, and come back to it daily to start
developing fluency. This should not hurt, so slow down
and take breaks if you feel tension.

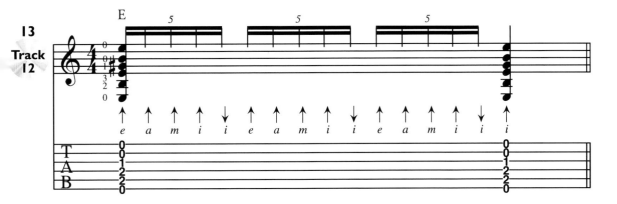

Arpeggio

The word *arpeggio* is translated as "broken chord." An arpeggio is created when we play the notes of a chord one by one rather than simultaneously. This is a very popular technique on the guitar and was used heavily in classical guitar repertoire prior to being incorporated into flamenco technique. There are endless possible permutations of the arpeggio, though there are a few that are prevalent in flamenco.

Placement of right-hand fingers.

The arpeggios we will look at in this section all feature the consecutive use of the *p, i, m,* and *a* fingers. Let's start the arpeggio by placing the right-hand fingers on their respective strings. We'll place *p* on the 6th string, *i* on the 3rd string, *m* on the 2nd string, and *a* on the 1st string. See photo to the right.

Notice the angle of the wrist. We gain support for the hand by resting our fingertips on the strings. Make sure not to support the hand by bending the wrist toward, or by resting on, the face of the guitar.

Squeeze all four strings a couple of times, observing how the strings feel. Look at your hand to take a visual survey of the spacing between the strings and how your fingers fall on the strings.

Now, with a slight clockwise twisting motion, like turning a car key, pluck all four strings together. This way of plucking chords is not an arpeggio but is used in flamenco and other styles of music, as well—most notably Brazilian styles of guitar. The feel of this type of plucking is the reference point for the feel of the arpeggio.

Using our now familiar chord sequence (but with slightly different chord voicings), practice this chord technique. Note that in the first measure, your thumb is playing the 5th string rather than the 6th.

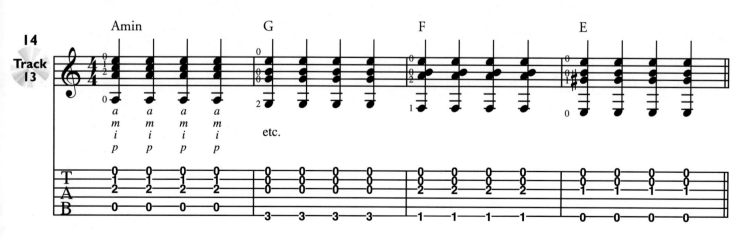

"Peeling"

Now try the exact same motion, but let the thumb release a bit before the others. Rolling the thumb away from the guitar, let the fingers follow behind the thumb, thus "peeling" off of the strings one by one. This should feel like the same single motion just used in the chord technique, though by starting with the thumb, a kind of peeling effect takes place, like removing a piece of tape from a surface, and the fingers wind up plucking the notes one by one—an arpeggio!

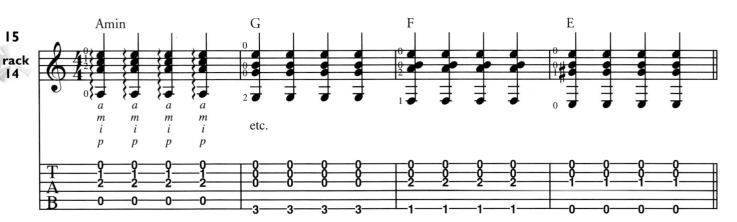

Now, do the same exercise in reverse, starting the movement with the pinky. Although the pinky is not touching any strings, by moving it toward the palm, the other fingers will be inclined to follow along. (See Figs. 1–5 below.)

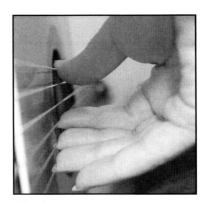

Fig. 1.

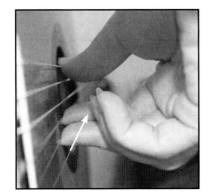

Fig. 2.

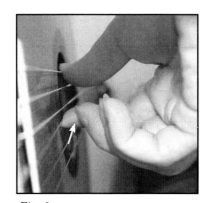

Fig. 3.

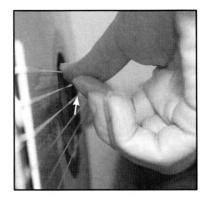

Fig. 4.

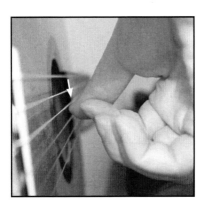

Fig. 5.

On page 35, we will be playing an arpeggio example that is a combination of the two peeled arpeggios above. However, we need to look a little more closely at the free stroke before we try it.

Free Stroke

We've been using the free stroke for our plucking and peeling, so let's focus on this technique a bit more before moving on to the example on the next page.

A good free stroke requires solid contact with the string and then a relaxed movement of the fingertip. The thumb can stand by to stabilize the fingertip until it gets used to this movement, similar to the way the adjacent string is used in rest stroke. (See photos below.)

A good free stroke requires solid contact with the string and then a relaxed movement of the fingertip. The thumb can stand by to stabilize the fingertip until it gets used to this movement.

Now, let's work on our free stroke by playing the individual open strings with each right-hand finger, then alternating between the *i* and *m* fingers. Concentrate on comfort and tone.

 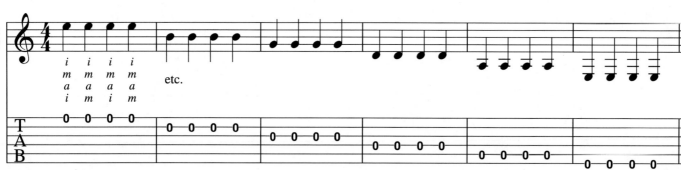

In this exercise, we develop the independent movement of the thumb required for the alternating bass notes frequently used in an arpeggio. While you use the thumb to play the notes, place the *i, m,* and *a* fingers on the strings as though they are about to play the arpeggio (like we did with the plucking and peeling exercises on the previous pages) and keep them there throughout the exercise.

Play each measure 4 times

The example below is a combination of the two types of peeled arpeggios we did on page 33, connected with a sort of pivot at the ring finger. It can be thought of as a peel forward of *p–i–m*, and then a peel back of *a–m–i*. As you play this example, concentrate on good free-stroke technique.

Chapter 3:
Compás—The Heartbeat of Flamenco

The numerous flamenco song forms (palos) can be grouped in many different ways: by place of origin, emotional character, scales used, etc. One of the most obvious ways is to make two groups—forms with a regular rhythmic pulse, or compás, and the rhythmically free forms known as cantes libres (or toques libres).

In the rhythmic palos, the importance of maintaining the given compás structure cannot be over-emphasized. Flamenco music is, among many things, profoundly groove-driven. The importance of internalizing the rhythms, so that the music you play is naturally carried along by an unwavering and vibrant sense of compás, is central to being a fine player. This is certainly true of the solo player, and it becomes utterly indispensable when playing with others, whether they are guitarists, singers, dancers, or percussionists. Compás is the lingua franca (common language) of flamenco. It is what allows successful communication between all parties, and once internalized, serves as the foundation for ever-expanding interpretive possibilities and creative variations.

Flamenco without strong and fluid compás is like a body without bones; it simply doesn't work, even if all the other components are in good shape.

Other Meanings of Compás

The word compás is used for a number of things in flamenco, and we learn a great deal about flamenco by looking at the different applications of this word. First, compás is used to refer to the specific rhythmic pattern used in a given palo. Some forms use a twelve-beat compás pattern (soleá, bulerías, siguiriyas), others use a six-beat pattern (fandango de huelva, sevillanas), and still others use a four-beat pattern (tangos, rumba, etc.). So, for example, the "compás of tangos" refers to the specific four-beat pattern used in tangos.

Next, compás can be used to mean the same as the musical term "measure" in English, as in, one measure of music. One compás is one measure, or one time through the rhythmic cycle of whichever palo you're playing (four beats or six beats, etc.).

Finally, compás refers to an aspect of musicality, as in he/she has "good compás." This use of the word implies a freedom to do expressive, or musically inspiring or supportive, things within the specific compás structure. This last definition, of course, requires a deep internalization of the mechanical aspects of compás, so that one hears and feels the rhythms internally and has the basic rhythm flowing out of them.

The aim of this chapter is to develop not only a knowledge of the specific compáses and the palos they're associated with, but also to provide, with the help of the CD, a method for gaining greater internalization of the rhythms. The exercises in this chapter, as with the Technique Survival Kit, can be used again and again to go ever deeper into this art form. The simplicity of these exercises is what gives them their power. The repetition of the individual patterns allows the rhythms to soak into your ear and hand, so that more and more, week after week, these rhythms become internalized.

While flamenco has over 50 palos, it is useful to realize that the vast majority of the forms can all be connected to one of four primary rhythmic types. In this section, we will learn these four primary rhythmic structures and begin applying them to the various palos that they help define.

Below are the four compás types and some associated palos.

1. **Three- and six-beat rhythms.** Some palos that use these rhythms are fandangos, sevillanas, and verdiales.

2. **Four-beat rhythms.** Tangos, rumbas, colombianas, and farrucas are in this group.

3. **Twelve-beat family I.** Soleás, alegrías, and bulerías belong to this category.

4. **Twelve-beat family II.** Palos in this group include siguiriyas, serranas, and martinetes.

Three- and Six-Beat Rhythms

The three- and six-beat rhythms come first because they are all-pervasive in Andalucian culture. There are many non-flamenco song forms that use the rhythms from this family, and the strong three-beat pulse is deeply embedded in the Andalucian psyche. On its own, the basic three-beat rhythm is used in numerous song forms, but it is also an underlying part of most of the twelve-beat rhythmic patterns used in flamenco. The basic three-beat pattern (see page 39, Example 20) is clapped by audiences at public events like soccer matches, bullfights, and concerts—not to mention, it is the rhythm of choice for many of the most emblematic folk dances, such as the sevillanas and fandangos, as well as being used for villancicos (Christmas carols). Many of these forms have phrases in pairs of threes, in other words, six-beat phrases; hence, the combination of three- and six-beat rhythms in this same group.

The power of this rhythm is felt when in a room (or stadium) filled with people doing it all together. One is swept up by the powerful pulsation that is created. Those who grow up feeling this have the rhythm rooted in their core. Through a great deal of listening and practice, it is possible to internalize this pulse within yourself as well.

Ramón Montoya (1880–1949) is considered the father of solo flamenco guitar, in many ways creating the template for all flamenco guitarists that followed him. A preeminent accompanist in his era, his incorporation of techniques such as arpeggio and tremolo (gained from his association with classical guitar maestro Miguel Llobet) led him to expand the possibilities of flamenco guitar. Montoya was among the very first to create and perform virtuoso solo flamenco guitar music in concerts and recitals, leading to a new era in the evolution of flamenco guitar.

Our first step in learning the three- and six-beat rhythms will be to practice a strumming technique in which the left hand mutes the strings. This results in an unpitched, percussive sound rather than the clear notes of a chord and is referred to as playing with the *cuerdas tapadas* (covered strings). Sometimes, it is referred to as just *tapadas* or *tapada* (covered), or *seco* (dry).

Tapada technique is used all the time. Frequently, it is a way to set up the rhythm at the beginning of a piece, or it is used as a percussive interlude in the middle of a piece. It can also create contrasting sections and rhythmic interplay with dancers, and is frequently used throughout an entire piece as percussive accompaniment for other guitarists and/or singers and dancers.

Now, let's try to play with cuerdas tapadas. Making a loose fist with the right hand, and covering the strings with the left hand around the 9th and 10th frets, strum through the strings a few times, all at once, with your fingertips. Listen for a crisp, even sound. (See photo below.)

Cuerdas Tapadas.

Now, try the same thing with the four-finger rasgueado.

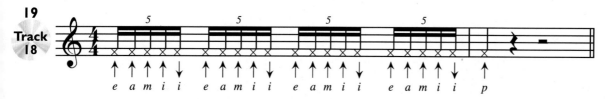

Practicing the Six-Beat Rhythms

Following are two versions of the rhythms used in the six-beat family. The first is the most basic version and is really just pairs of three-beat cycles. It is played with a downstrum of the *i* finger on each beat, followed by the rasgueado on the offbeats (the "ands") of beats 1 and 2.

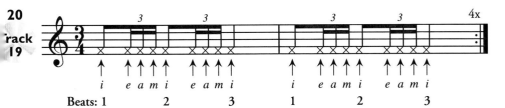

Track 20 consists of a rhythm track that can be used to practice the tapada sequence above.

The following full six-beat pattern is nearly the same as the pattern above, though we rest on the last beat and do not play the rasgueado on beat 2 of the second measure. Accents fall on beats 1 and 2.

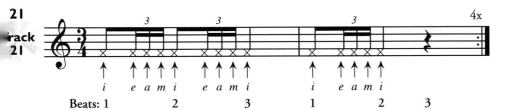

Following are two rhythm tracks for practicing the six-beat tapada. Track 22 is a slow version and Track 23 is a fast version. Take your time with the slow version before moving on to Track 23.

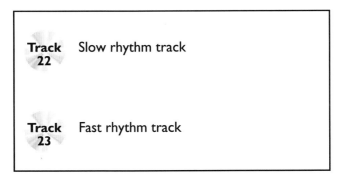

Track 22 Slow rhythm track

Track 23 Fast rhythm track

Practice the preceding patterns along with the CD—or to recordings of fandangos de Huelva (see below)—to help develop fluency. Make sure to practice slowly at first and to take breaks if you feel tension. As always, remember to keep breathing. Breathing is usually the first thing to go when we are a little uncertain of what we are doing, and this leads directly to tension in the body. So, remember to keep checking in on your breathing.

Fandangos de Huelva

The *fandango* is one of the most popular forms in Spanish folk dance and music. Its origins are suggested to be as far back as ancient Roman times, and this form has spawned many variations. Some of these have made their way into flamenco, most notably the *fandangos de Huelva* (from the province of Huelva, south of Portugal), as well as the *fandango de Málaga*, also known as *verdiales*. There are many non-rhythmic variations, such as the *fandangos libres* (free fandangos) and many regional variations, including the *malagueña* from Málaga, the *granaína* from Granada, and the various mining songs from the areas of Almería and Murcia, such as the *taranta, minera,* and *cartegenera.*

Below is the signature chord sequence and rhythm for the fandangos de Huelva.

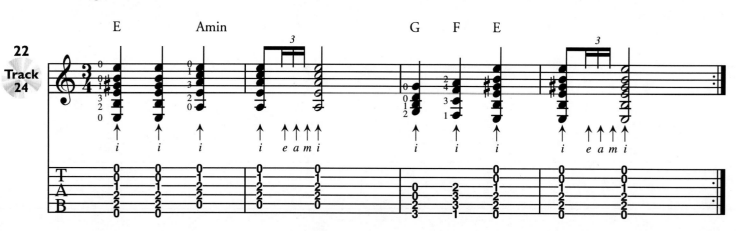

The above sequence should be repeated again and again, first to develop smooth chord transitions, then to make sure all the notes sound clear. Once these are in place, full attention goes to infusing the sequence with a strong sense of the six-beat pulse we've been working on. Here, it may be useful to go back and practice the tapada version some more.

Below is a longer selection. This material can be used to set up a *solo piece* (guitar alone), *dance version* (guitar accompaniment for a dancer), or song version (guitar accompaniment for a singer) of the fandangos de Huelva.

Here, we introduce the upstroke with the *i* finger in alternation with the downstroke (see beats 2 and 3 of measures 2 and 6, and all three beats of measure 5). For the upstroke, simply place the finger on the high E and "wipe" upward (see Figs. 1 and 2 below).

Fig. 1.

Fig. 2.

The E7 Chord

In addition, we will be playing an E7 chord in measure 5, which is just like an E chord but with an open 4th string. Check out the fingering to the right, and then try Example 23.

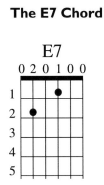

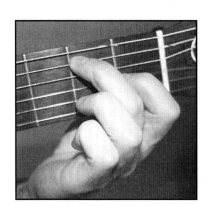

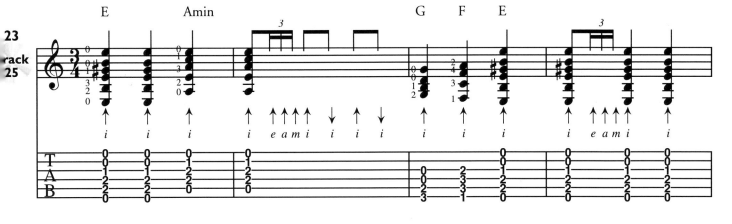

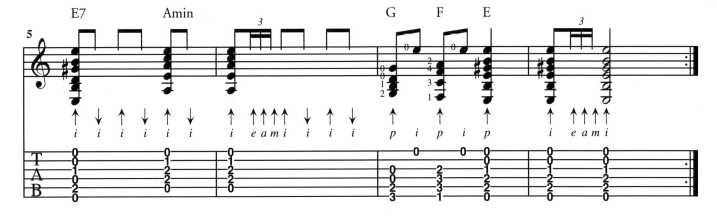

Four-Beat Rhythms: Tangos

The four-beat rhythmic cycle is certainly the most prevalent in Western musical culture, whether it be in classical, jazz, rock, pop, or hip-hop. Several of the most popular flamenco palos also use a four-beat cycle, such as tangos, tientos, and rumba. Here, we will look at the *tangos* rhythm, which is closely related to these other forms.

As we mute the strings with the left hand, we see the pattern is identical to the three-beat sequence in the previous section, with one additional downstroke on the fourth beat.

> = *Accent.* Emphasize this note or chord.

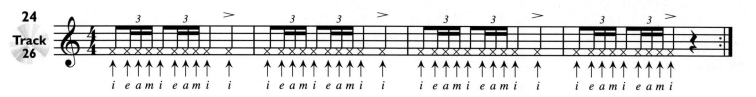

Practice the tapada sequence above along with the following rhythm tracks.

> **Track 27** Slow rhythm track
>
> **Track 28** Fast rhythm track

Tangos is one of the lively *cantes festeros* (festive songs) of flamenco. It is traditionally sung at Gypsy weddings and other festive occasions. The strong four-beat compás has been used to create flamenco songs that, at times, cross over to more mainstream audiences. Along with the rumba, tangos is regarded as more accessible to the general population than some other types of flamenco. Like most of the song forms, it has numerous regional variations, most notably the tangos from Extremadura (an autonomous community in Spain encompassing the provinces of Cáceres and Badajoz), Triana (a neighborhood in Seville), and the city of Granada.

Example 25 is a basic tangos compás. Notice the *golpe* (indicated with the symbol x) in measure 4; this technique is covered on page 63. We also need to look at two new chords: A and B♭. To play the A chord, you need to use the *barring* technique, which is covered on page 72.

The A Chord

The B♭ Chord

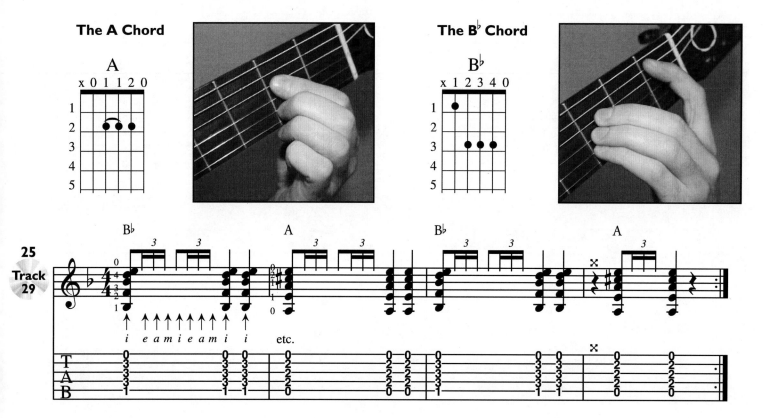

Tangos Falseta

Notice in the basic thumb falseta below how we introduce single notes into the tangos rhythm. Understanding the connection between basic compás and falseta playing is an absolute key to playing in a way that exudes the pulse rather than temporarily departing from it. In other words, even an elaborate falseta is a compás delivery mechanism. It don't mean a thing if it ain't got that swing in flamenco!

26
Track 30

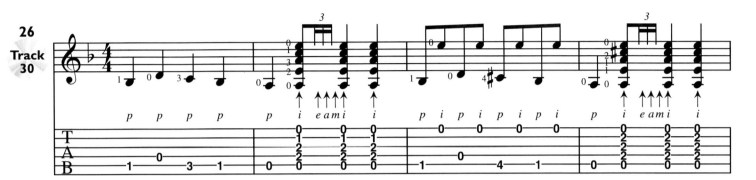

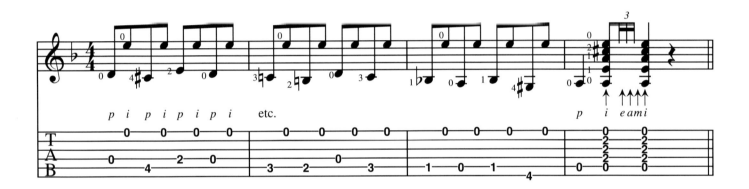

Tangos Compás Variations

On the next page, there are a couple of variations on the basic tangos compás. To play them, we need to look at two more chords: D Minor (Dmin) and C7. Acquaint yourself with the fingerings below, then try the examples on the next page.

The D Minor Chord

Dmin
x x 0 2 3 1

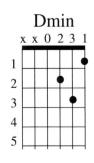

The C7 Chord

C7
x 3 2 4 1 0

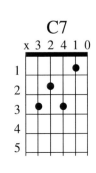

Tangos Compás—Variation 1

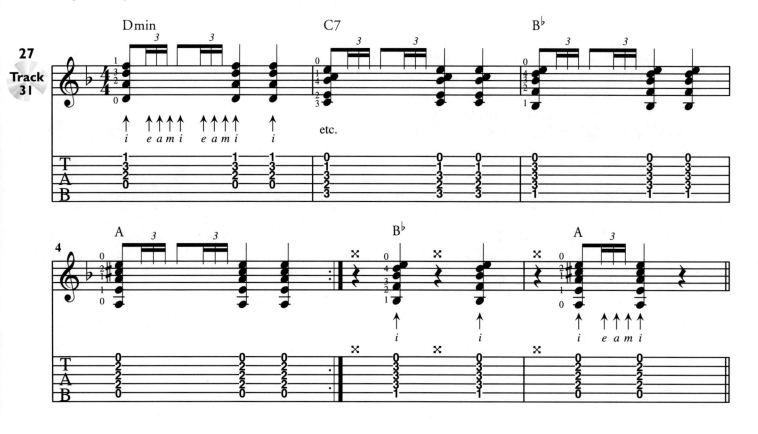

Tangos Compás—Variation 2

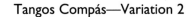

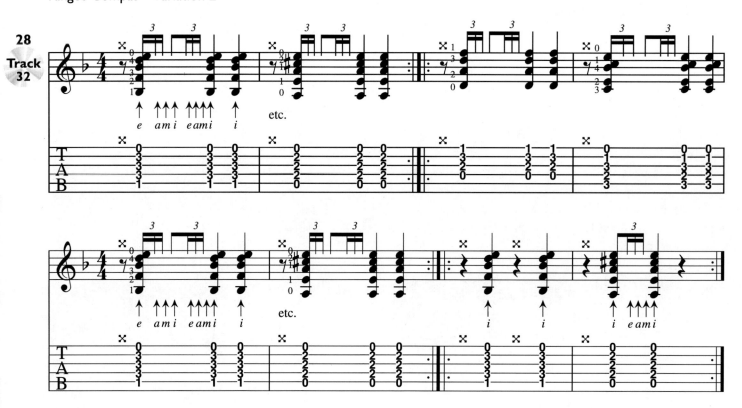

Now, let's look at an arpeggio example that would be played to a tangos compás.

Twelve-Beat Compás Family I: Soleá, Soleá por Bulerías, Alegrías, and Bulerías

The palos in this family are central to flamenco. Along with the tangos and siguiriyas, these form the heart of what is regarded as gypsy flamenco song—a primary ingredient in flamenco, and considered by some to be the only true flamenco forms. These palos all relate to one another because they share the same basic accent patterns within the twelve-beat cycle. The *soleá* is the oldest of all these forms, as well as the slowest and most emotionally profound. It is also referred to as *soleares*, which is an Andalucian pronunciation of the word *soledad*, meaning "solitude." The *alegrías* and *bulerías* are generally much faster and are outright festive forms, with the *soleá por bulerías* having a medium tempo and somewhat serious character—falling right in between the soleá and the other forms on the emotional spectrum.

While much subtle variation can occur between the different palos in this family, let's look at the most typical ways this rhythm is counted.

There are two very standard ways of playing this compás that are nearly identical, with the exception of one differing accent.

Internalizing the Twelves

Try tapping out the following sequence several times in a row on the face of your guitar or a tabletop. The numbers in bold represent the accented beats in the cycle. You will notice the first beat in this sequence starts on 12 and not 1. This is an interesting aspect to the way this rhythm is counted. Many of the musical phrases in these forms do actually start on beat 1, though it is not an accented beat. Since the 12 is accented, it easily takes over the 1 in terms of hearing it as the starting point. The musical examples that follow in this section all start with beat 1, though if they were to be repeated or looped, you would feel the natural starting point as beat 12. This rhythm existed before it was ever counted, so the counting—as always in flamenco—is a later attempt to describe what was already going on in the music. While counting from 12 can seem confusing at first, with repetition, it will become quite natural. Let's try it.

Track 34
12 1 2 **3** 4 5 **6** 7 **8** 9 **10** 11 (**12** 1 2 **3** etc.)

The next pattern is equally common in all of the twelve-beat forms. Notice that the only difference between this pattern and the one on the previous page is the shift of the accent from beat 6 to beat 7. This change does, however, give a distinct rhythmic flavor. For contrast and variety, many pieces feature frequent transitions back and forth between the two patterns. Practice tapping this rhythm along with Tracks 35–37.

12 1 2 **3** 4 5 6 **7** **8** 9 **10** 11 (**12** 1 2 **3** etc.)

Track 35 Slow rhythm track   **Track 36** Medium rhythm track   **Track 37** Fast rhythm track

Below are two variations of soleá compás. As always, you want to repeat each of these measures (remember, in this context, the term "measure" implies the entire twelve-beat cycle) 20, 50, even 100 times in a session (as long as you stay loose and keep breathing). This will help you integrate the rhythm, technique, and tone into your body. The best playing comes from no longer having to think about the basics, and this can only result from a real immersion in those basics. Note that this is the first example that uses *ligado* (hammer-ons, pull-offs, etc.). See page 59 for more on this smooth, connected way of playing notes.

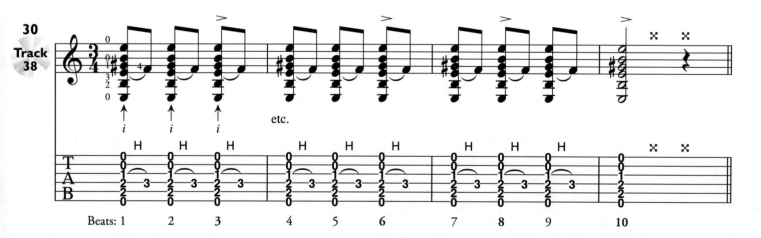

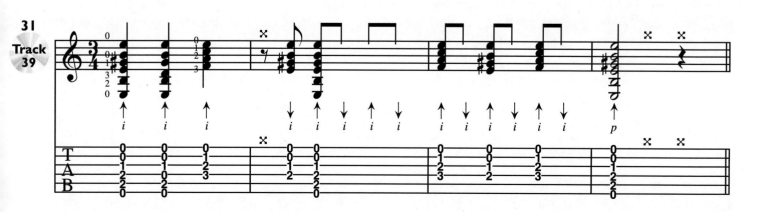

Following is a classic sequence of soleá, which features many of the techniques, chords, and rhythms we've been covering.

Soleá Sequence

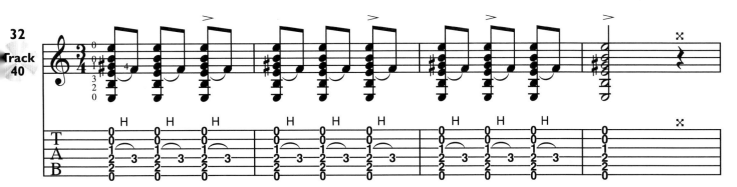

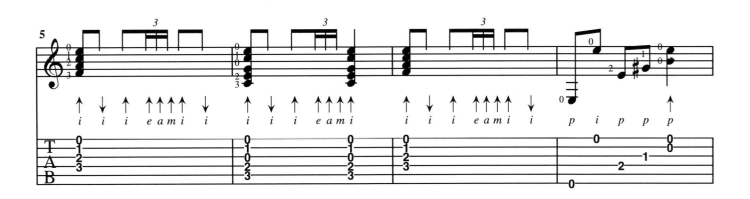

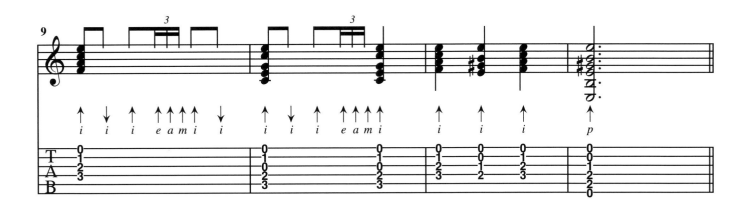

Alegrías

The *alegrías* is one of the few forms in flamenco to use a diatonic major tonality (the major scale consists of scale degrees 1–2–3–4–5–6–7), whereas much of flamenco uses the Phrygian mode we looked at earlier. This major scale is very common in Western classical music and is considered to have a happy or bright sound, certainly in comparison to the minor feel of the Phrygian mode most often used in flamenco. Indeed, the word "alegrías" means "joy" or "happiness," which is reflected not only in the use of the major tonality but also in the relatively faster tempo of the form.

To get us in the flavor of the *alegrías*, let's first practice the E Major scale. Not only does this root our ear firmly in the sound of *alegrías*, but it prepares us for the frequent use of scale passages in this form.

E Major Scale

The B7 Chord

You will notice in the following alegrias compás that the rhythmic pattern is identical to what we've already learned in the soleá. Repeat this until the transitions are smooth and the rhythm is very clear. There is one new chord in this example: B7 (really a B11 chord, but we will think of it as a voicing for B7).

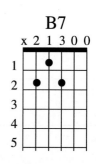

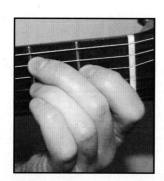

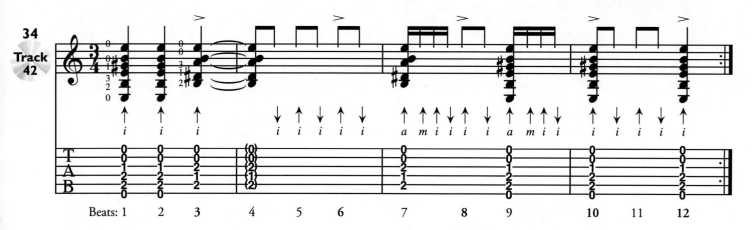

In this more extended passage, we learn a few new rhythmic variations and a thumb falseta. Additionally, this example features the first appearance of the golpe and a chord played simultaneously, a technique covered on page 64.

Alegrías Sequence

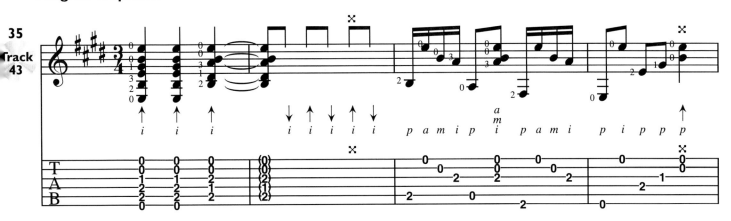

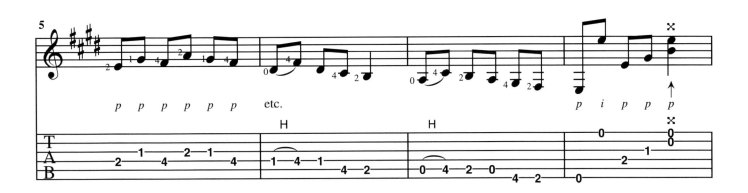

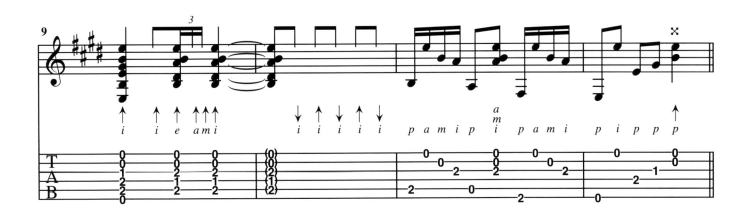

Twelve-Beat Family II: The Siguiriyas

While the *siguiriyas* and the related forms of cabales, serranas, and martinetes all use a twelve-beat compás, the typical way this is counted is in five, relating to the five accented beats in the compás cycle. The songs in this family are amongst the most profound and *jondo* (deep) of all the flamenco forms. They are greatly associated with the gypsy *fraguas* (blacksmith forges), where day in and day out—while pounding out nails, horseshoes, and the like—the blacksmith would sing these songs accompanied only by the clinking of the hammer on the anvil. This helps explain the droning, almost eternal and profound nature of these songs, where the singer often sings about their greatest pain and loss. The martinete does not use guitar accompaniment and to this day is often performed *a capella* (voice alone) or is accompanied only by a hammer tapping on an anvil—or a cane tapping out the compás.

The rhythm looks like this:

I 2 **3** 4 **5** 6 7 **8** 9 10 **II** 12

but is counted like this:

I and **2** and **3** and ah **4** and ah **5** and

Notice that the numbers I through 5 in the second version correspond exactly to the accented numbers I, 3, 5, 8, and II in the first version. These two rhythms are identical, but the second is the most common way to count it. Get used to this rhythm by counting and clapping it out along with Tracks 44 and 45.

| **Track 44** | Slow rhythm track | **Track 45** | Fast rhythm track |

The example below demonstrates the standard compás of the siguiriyas. Notice the time signature ($\frac{3}{4}+\frac{6}{8}$), which indicates an alternation between $\frac{3}{4}$ and $\frac{6}{8}$ every measure. In $\frac{3}{4}$, there are three beats per measure, with the quarter note receiving the beat (1-&, 2-&, 3-&). In $\frac{6}{8}$, there are six beats per measure, with the eighth note receiving the beat. Typically, however, $\frac{6}{8}$ is counted with the pulse on the dotted quarter note (1-&-ah, 2-&-ah). Be sure to listen to the CD to get the feel of this tricky rhythm.

36

Track 46

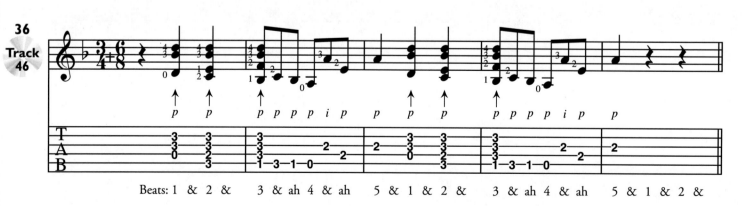

Beats: 1 & 2 & 3 & ah 4 & ah 5 & 1 & 2 & 3 & ah 4 & ah 5 & 1 & 2 &

As always, repeat the preceding example for several minutes to improve fluency and tone—and especially important in the seguiriya, to develop a sense of weight and grandeur that is integral to the spirit of this palo.

Here are some more variations of the siguiriyas compás.

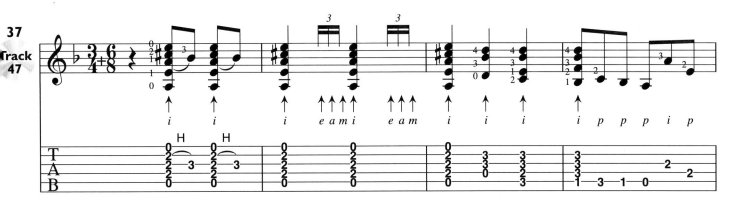

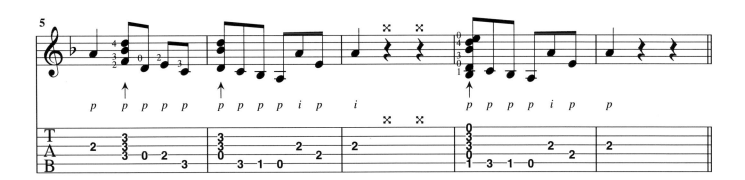

Congratulations! You have now learned about all the basic rhythmic groups in flamenco. The significance of this is tremendous. While there are variations on all of these rhythms, with the information learned in this chapter, you have a reference and entry point for every rhythmic flamenco song you'll ever hear!

Chapter 4:
Putting It All Together—First Solos

In this chapter, we bring together and build upon all the concepts and material covered so far. The four selections in this chapter have two purposes:

1. To further develop your vocabulary of rhythmic variations in four of the main flamenco palos (siguiriyas, soleá, bulerías, and tangos)

2. To begin building a performance repertoire by incorporating some falsetas into the selections

Both in structure and technique, the pieces in this chapter embody all of the important elements of most flamenco repertoire you will encounter. Therefore, practicing these selections with a focus on rhythmic fluency and good tone will prove very beneficial.

When practicing the material in this section, it is important to understand that, traditionally, in both accompaniment and solo playing, the rhythmic sections between verses or falsetas are improvised. So, a player may have dozens of slight variations—practiced beforehand—on the basic chordal sequences. While playing a piece, the guitarist is free to spontaneously choose the variations they feel best for that particular moment. The development of your own repertoire of variations is one of the most important aspects in your development as a flamenco guitarist.

Siguiriyas

In our first solo, we see some familiar, as well as new, variations on the basic siguiriyas compás. Learning these well will give you a great variety of rhythmic variations and will be useful to you when learning the full siguiriyas solo later in the book (page 93).

Track 48 *Siguiriyas*

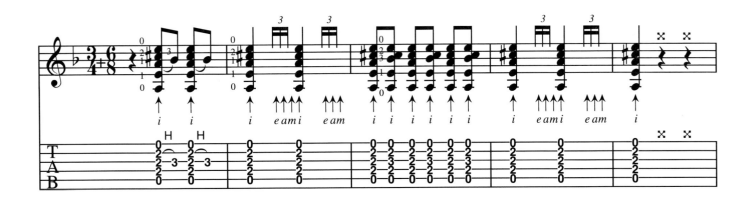

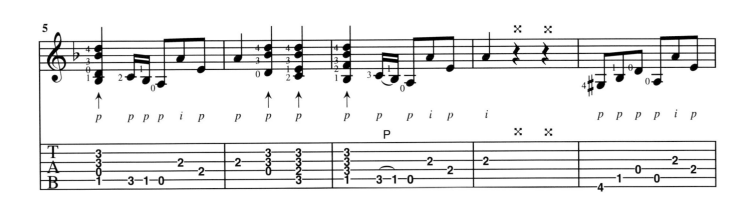

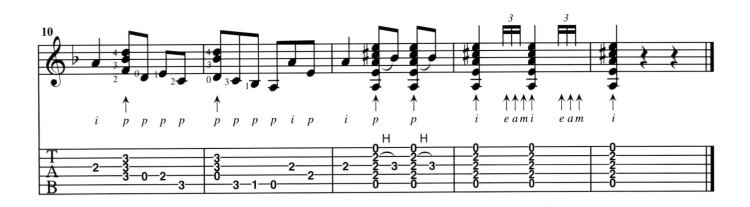

Soleá

The soleá below shows several of the most important compás variations for this palo, while also featuring a range of techniques. The falseta starting in measure 21 provides an opportunity to work on your thumb technique, while demonstrating a typical rhythmic structure that could be used as a starting point in a soleá falseta—or on its own as written.

Track 49 *Soleá*

Tangos

In this solo, we explore more variations of the tangos compás, along with a picado and thumb falseta. Thorough practice of all of these lessons will help you adapt even more variations. As you learn these, you will come to recognize them when attending live flamenco performances or listening to recordings.

Track 50 *Tangos*

Bulerías: Four Ways of Playing the Compás

As mentioned at the beginning of this chapter, a flamenco guitarist should work on developing not only fluency in the material they learn, but the ability to spontaneously mix and match the order of the compáses they use.

The next page features four different ways to play the bulerías compás. Practice each of them individually until smooth. After that, begin to play them one after the other—first in the order they appear, then in different orders. It is recommended that you use the bulerías rhythm tracks (Tracks 35–37) on the companion CD as you practice. Make sure to start with the slow version first!

Following is a brief description of each of the four compás examples on the next page.

- Example 38 is a good introductory bulerías compás.

- Example 39 uses the $^\flat$9 voicing for the A chord covered on page 69. This is one of the most common and distinctively "flamenco" sounding chords.

- Example 40 is a traditional variation of the bulerías compás.

- Example 41 uses the same right-hand figures as Example 38, but cycles through the chords B$^\flat$, C9, B$^\flat$, and A. This is a very characteristic progression that can be used as an ending, or to help prepare the ear for a new phrase or section.

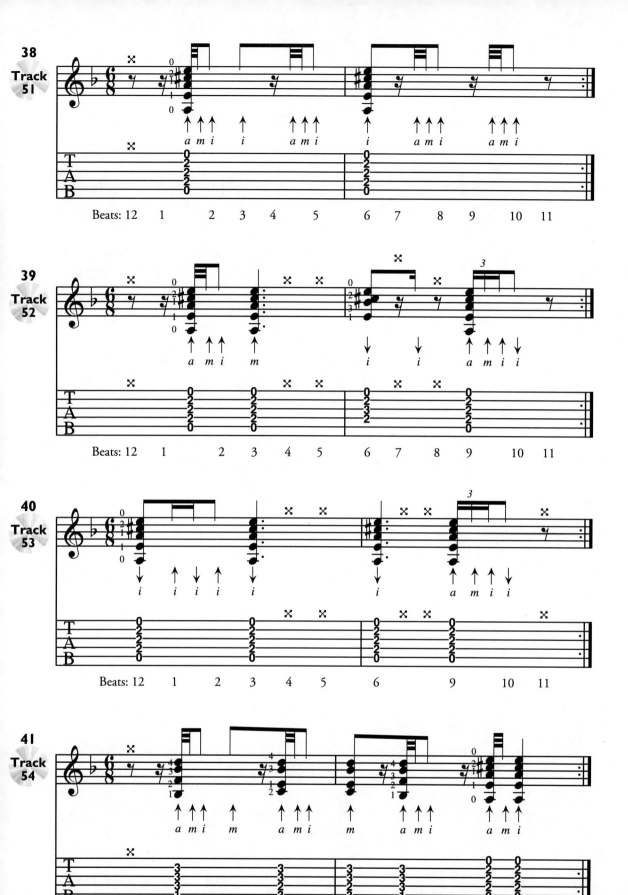

As mentioned earlier, flamenco is profoundly dependent on a solid internalization of the rhythms we have been looking at. This point cannot be stressed enough. That being said, now that we have looked at all of the basic rhythmic types, a little secret about flamenco is that the reason the style is so evolved and people attain such great levels of internalized rhythm is because they are always drawing from this same small pool of rhythms. So, over the course of months and years of practicing and listening, you are able to delve deeper and deeper into these same fundamental sets of rhythms, rather than having to learn new ones.

Chapter 5: Additional Techniques

In the Technique Survival Kit (see page 17), we looked at the fundamental techniques needed to start playing real music. However, flamenco guitar utilizes an array of additional techniques as well, which we will look at in this chapter.

Some Practice Pointers

As always, approach the material in this chapter with a relaxed and patient attitude. Remember that real progress comes over time to those who practice daily (or at least 5–6 days per week). It is not recommended to practice technique only for more than two or three hours per day; keep in mind that even 15–45 minutes can yield good results. Regardless of how much you practice, make sure you stay relaxed, letting your arms hang by your side for several seconds between each exercise and standing up regularly. It is also recommended to take a 10–15 minute break after every 45 minutes of practice.

Ligado: Hammer-Ons and Pull-Offs

Ligado (which means smooth, connected) is a technique where you play groups of notes without plucking with the right hand. All the notes are sounded with the left hand alone, using *pull-offs* and *hammer-ons*. Playing ligado is often viewed as more advanced and/or strenuous to the hand, but when approached properly, it can feel quite natural. Legato passages are connected with curved line called a *slur* ⌢ .

Pull-Offs

To execute a pull-off, pull your finger downward—or off of—a fretted note, thereby sounding a second note on the same string; this second note needs to be already fretted, or you can pull off to the open string itself.

Let's build up to this technique by plucking the open high-E string with each finger of the left hand, one at a time. This will give us the feel for both hammering-on and pulling-off.

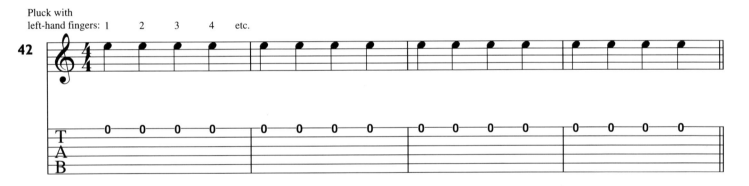

Next, you will be pulling off from a fretted, plucked note. For example, In the first measure, fret the A note with your left hand and pluck it with your right, then pull off with your left-hand finger to sound the open E string, and repeat the process. Try to maintain a consistent volume between the first and second notes of each pull-off.

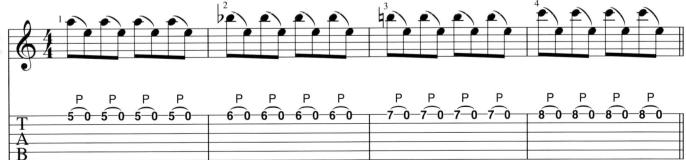

Hammer-Ons

A hammer-on is executed by dropping the weight of the fingertip onto the string at a particular fret to sound a note. You can hammer-on from another note, or just hammer-on to the note you want to sound, with no preceding note (sometimes, we call this a hammer-on-from-nowhere). This is the technique we will use in the next exercise (which also features pull-offs). For example, in measure 1,

hammer-on to the A note by dropping your fingertip to the 5th fret, thereby sounding the first quarter note. Then, pluck the second quarter note with the right hand. Now, pull your finger down—or off of—the A note, thereby sounding the open E string, etc.

$\underset{\frown}{\text{H}}$ = Hammer-on

Play each measure 4 times

44
Track 56

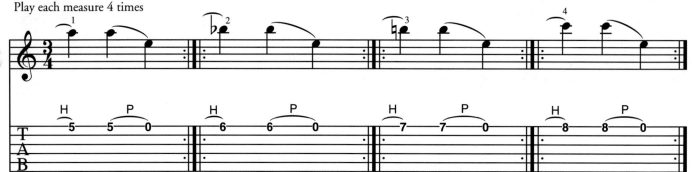

How Does the Fingertip Create the Sound in the Pull-Off?

While many people attempt pull-offs by retracting their finger, pulling it directly back away from the fretboard, the proper movement is really a miniature plucking with the tip. We use the flesh on the tip to grab the string, and, supported by the nail, move the finger tip in a slight rotation to grab and pluck the string. As always, the more relaxed you are, the more volume and richer the tone you will produce. This is just another way of plucking a note, equally important to plucking with the right hand. Check out the two photos to the right. Then, practice the following two exercises on all six strings.

Pull-off set-up.

Pull-off follow through.

45
Track 57

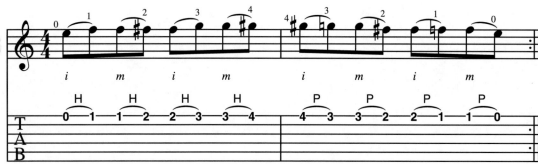

46
Track 58

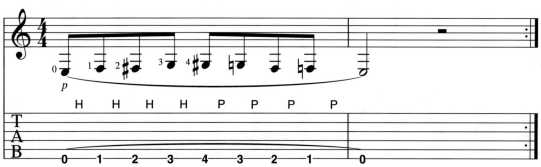

Abanico

There are many common variations of the rasgueado, with the *abanico* (used particularly in dance accompaniment) being the most common. This strumming technique was developed by the great Juan Maya "Marote," of Granada, one of Spain's greatest flamenco dance accompanists. The abanico is loved by guitarists for its combination of speed and power.

This technique is comprised of three parts:

1. Upstrum with the thumb ↓ *p*

2. Downstrum with the middle fingers ↑ *a* *m*

3. Downstroke with the thumb ↑ *p*

Performed slowly on open strings, it looks like this:

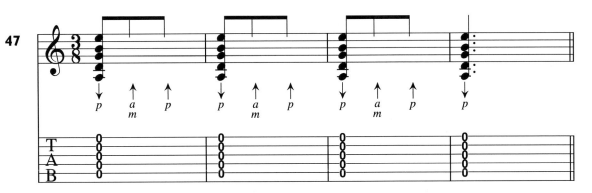

Because this is a three-stroke technique, it is used most often in passages with three- or six-notes per beat, with an accent on the first stroke of each group of three or six.

In the example below, the first stroke of every three is accented.

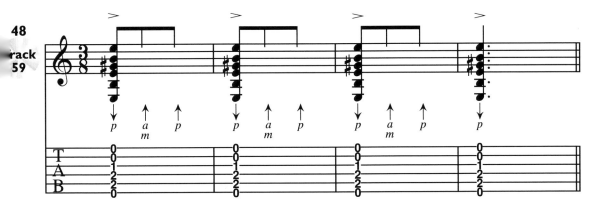

Below, the first stroke of every six is accented.

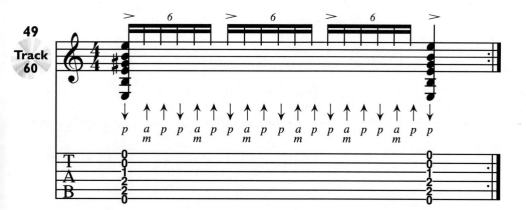

Following is an exercise you can add to your daily routine.
Do it slowly at first, listening for clarity in each stroke.

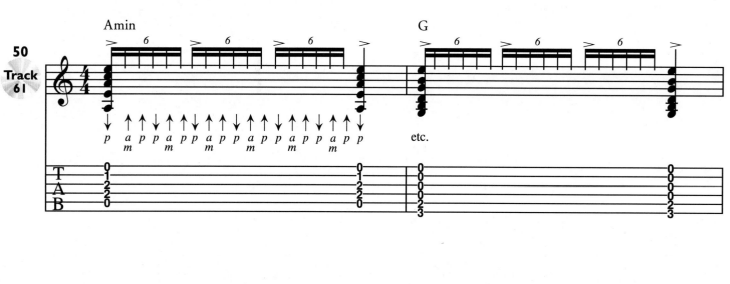

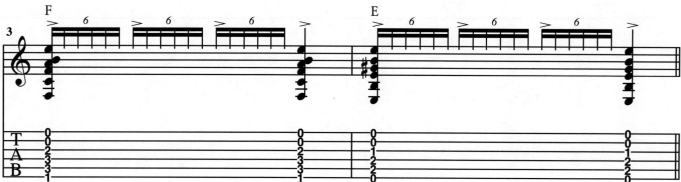

The Golpe

Golpear means to hit, or tap. This tapping is one of the signature sounds in flamenco, giving percussive emphasis throughout any of the rhythmic forms.

The basic technique is fairly simple, but as always, needs to done in a relaxed way allowing the weight of the hand to do the work.

The *golpe* is most often performed by either the ring finger alone or the ring and pinky fingers together; the fingers tap the face of the guitar below the strings, near the bridge. (See Fig. 1.)

Fig. 1.

Because of the internal bracing that holds the guitar together, there is great variety of tone produced depending on exactly where you tap. If you tap over a brace you get a much thinner sound, while tapping near the bridge produces a much deeper sound.

Using your ring finger, try tapping all around the face of the guitar to explore the wide range of sounds.

Fig. 2.

The nail is usually a part of the golpe's sound, and it is extremely important to hit from the underside of the nail, rather than driving the tip right into the guitar.

Try this:

1. Place the pad of the ring finger on the face of the guitar, and tap flesh only. Notice the dull thumping sound. (See Fig. 2.)

2. Now, roll the fingertip forward until the underside of the nail touches the guitar, and tap. You should hear the click of the nail, now blended with the thumping sound of the flesh. (See Fig. 3.)

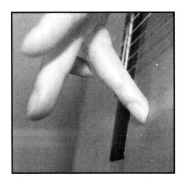

Fig. 3.

Approaching the golpe from this angle will save a lot of wear and tear on your nails!

Hand Position During Golpes

Normally, the thumb will be resting on the low-E string or face of the guitar, acting as a pivot point. If you rotate your wrist slightly upward, you can then drop the weight of the hand and get a very full sound. With practice, you can achieve the same by lifting and dropping just the finger. (See Figs. 4 and 5.)

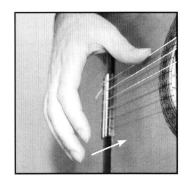

Fig. 4.

Fig. 5.

The Golpe in Action

The golpe is used one of two ways—either by itself between two chords or notes (as in Example 51), or together with a chord (as in Example 52).

Example 51 is a very basic rendering of the bulerías rhythm. (Notice the *1st and 2nd endings,* which tell you to play the 1st ending, then repeat as normal, skipping over the 1st ending and playing on from the 2nd ending.)

x = Golpe

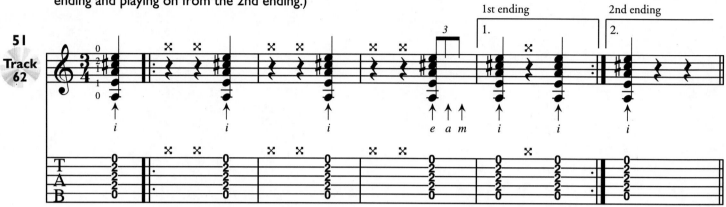

The strum and golpe together should feel like a single motion where you:

1. Retract the index finger to prepare for the strum

2. Pivot the hand, bringing the ring finger toward the guitar

3. Release the index finger as you pivot

When done properly, this feels no different than making the "so-so" gesture, tilting your hand from side to side. This combination of golpe and strum is extremely frequent, so you should get comfortable with it.

Below is a basic version of the soleá rhythm.

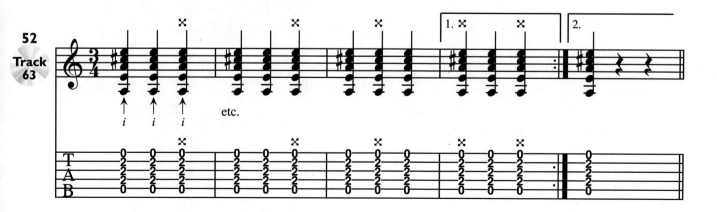

Alzapúa

The word *alzapúa* combines the Spanish words *alzar* (to go upward) and *pua* (thorn or cactus needle, as well as the Spanish word for guitar pick). When executed properly, the alzapua technique is an exciting and unique color in the flamenco guitarist's technical palette.

The alzapúa technique consists of alternating downward and upward strokes with the thumb only, although when done at its normal speed, it sounds like there are many fingers involved.

This technique has much in common with picking techniques used on the Arabic oud—the predecessor of the flamenco guitar, which presumably influenced the development of this characteristic flamenco technique.

The most common pattern used for alzapúa is three consecutive strokes—downward strum with thumb, upward strum with thumb, and single-note downstroke with thumb. Therefore, it is often used with triplet groupings or adds a fourth note using ligado technique in the left hand.

Below are examples of three- and four-note alzapúa patterns.

Three-Note Alzapúa Pattern

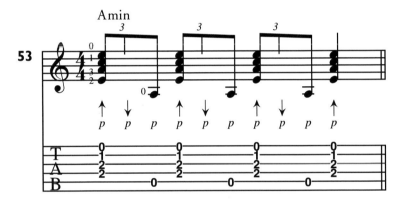

Four-Note Alzapúa Pattern

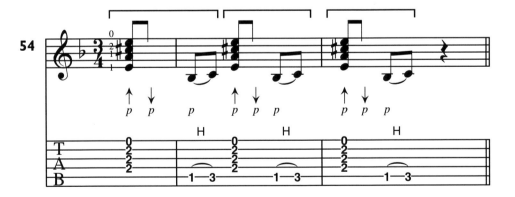

There are several very important things to know when developing a fluid, clear, and, ultimately, rhythmically powerful alzapúa. Most important are:

1. The angle of the thumb
2. Location of the other fingers
3. How to most effectively move the thumb, in order to develop tone, speed, precision, and ease

Angle of Thumb

Most players hold their thumb at an angle somewhere between 45 and 90 degrees to the strings. The angle used for alzapúa tends to be greater than that used when playing arpeggios, and it has the very important effect of directing the weight of the whole arm into the strings (see Fig. 1). This relaxed bending of the wrist allows a great amount of the work to be done for us.

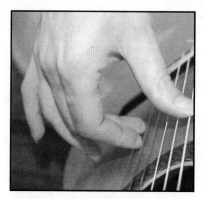

Fig. 1: Thumb angle for alzapúa.

To help you tap into all of the amazing arm weight available to us, try this: touch the pad of your thumb to the low-E string at a very low angle—10 degrees or so (see Fig. 2).

Fig. 2: 10 degree angle.

Now, as if the tip were glued to the string, slowly change the angle by lifting the wrist away from the guitar, moving towards 90 degrees. Notice that starting at around 45 degrees, the string starts to be pressed in more and more just by shifting the angle (see Figs. 3 and 4).

For the purposes of this exercise, it can be helpful to position the thumb over the soundhole, where the string is a little looser; though in actual playing, the position is typically between the rosette and the bridge.

Fig. 3: 45 degrees.

Position of the Rest of the Hand

As you can see in the photos on this page, the standard position for the other fingers when doing alzapúa is to have the index and middle finger touching the high-E string and face of the guitar for support, while the ring finger and pinky just relax.

Fig. 4: 90 degrees.

Developing Your Alzapúa

The alzapúa is like many of the techniques we use—a compound technique that actually combines three separate movements: downward strum with thumb, upward strum with thumb, and single-note downstroke with thumb.

As with any compound technique, the fastest way to gain proficiency is to develop each of the motions separately, instead of hoping they will all magically sound good in rapid sequence. So, make sure you can comfortably and consistently produce a good sound with each of the three components before starting serious practice of the alzapúa.

So far, we have worked on both the downward strum and single-note techniques with the thumb, which leaves the upward thumb strum. Let's look at that now.

The Upward Thumb Strum

The upward thumb strum can be practiced in much the same way as the downward strum. If we imagine using the strings to wipe something off the back of the thumbnail as we move across them, we will notice that we get quite a bit of sound.

For this to be performed correctly, the thumbnail needs to be completely smooth. So, if you are using artificial nail hardener—or even a fake nail—it must be very smooth and even, so as not to get even a little bit snagged.

Fig. 1.

At first, it is useful to lean the wrist toward the guitar, creating more contact with the thumbnail on the strings (see Fig. 1). This helps us to relax and feel the effect of the arm's weight. As we become more familiar with this technique, and move toward a finished alzapúa, the thumb becomes more perpendicular to the face of the guitar (see Fig. 2).

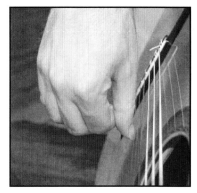

Fig. 2.

Now, let's practice the upward wiping motion eight times on the open strings, then on an E Major chord.

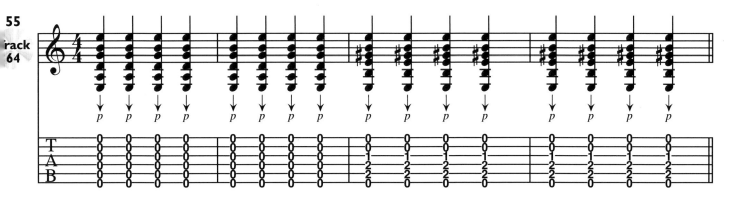

The next step is to practice alternating downward
and upward strums with the thumb, as in the example
below.

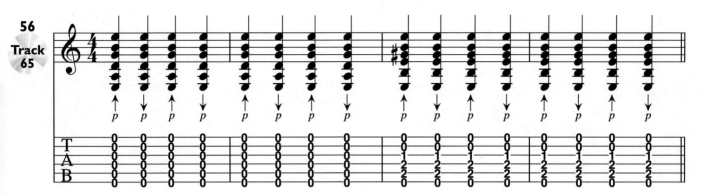

Now, let's add the single-note thumb stroke.

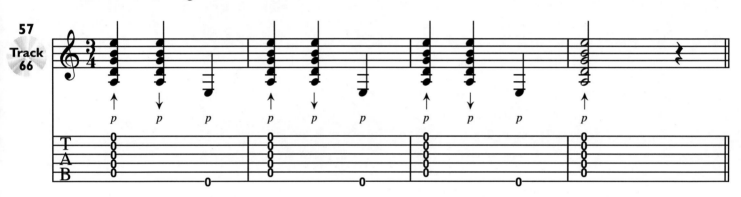

Here, we are using triplets to play a three-note alzapúa
pattern.

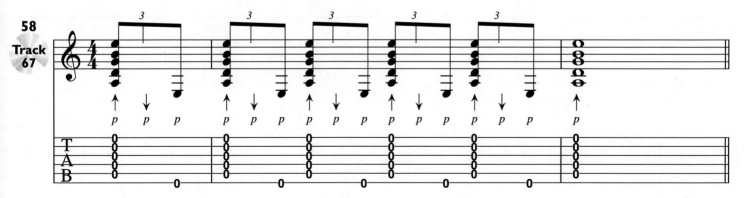

The thumb must stay relaxed at all times, which means we need to practice slowly at first, paying attention to the sound and relaxed feeling of every individual stroke.

Remember, we move the thumb from the large muscle in the palm, the thenar eminence. To the right, you'll see how the thumb should look in *neutral* position (the resting position before strumming) and in *contracted* position (the position after strumming).

Below is an alzapúa over a series chords.

Thumb in neutral position.

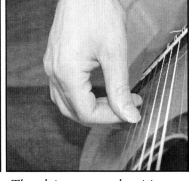
Thumb in contracted position.

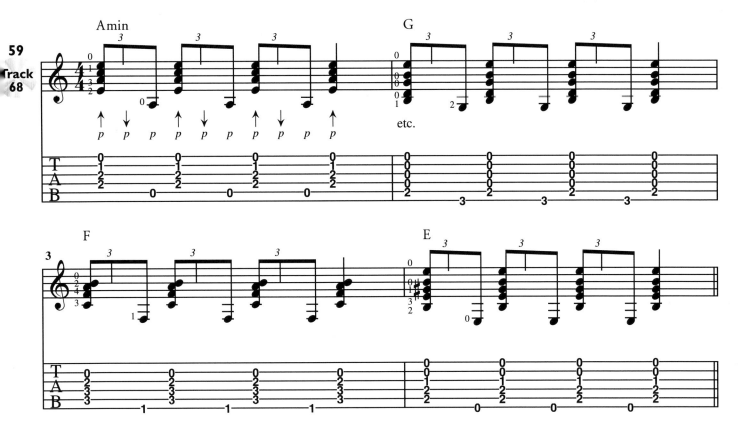

Following is an excerpt from the bulería piece on page 99, which incorporates ligado. This type of phrasing is very common, so practice it slowly until you are comfortable with it. This example also calls for a *capo* (see page 71) on the 3rd fret (Capo III). Additionally, there is a new chord in the last measure—a common flamenco "voicing" for an A chord, though, technically, it is an Aadd♭9.

Another Voicing for the A Chord

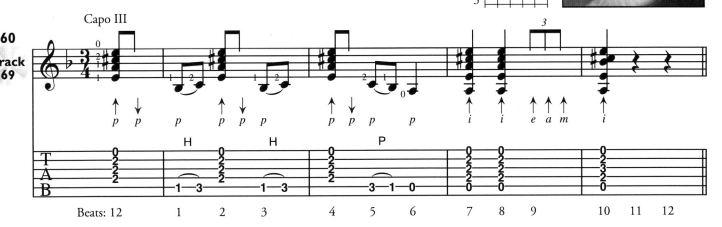

Tremolo

Tremolo is another technique adopted from classical guitar. It is as close to the voice or a bowed instrument as we can come on the guitar where, by rapid repetition of the same melodic note, we create the illusion of a continuous note. Tremolo is typically used for lyrical, flowing sections, and while, from the right hand, it resembles the arpeggio, it is a very unique-sounding technique.

The version of the tremolo most often used in flamenco is a five-note-per-beat technique consisting of the right-hand fingering: *p-i-a-m-i*. The classical tremolo, on the other hand, typically has one stroke less, consisting of *p-a-m-i*. The additional note in the flamenco tremolo adds density and lends itself to the intensity of flamenco music.

The tremolo uses rest stroke in the bass (thumb note) and free stroke in the repeating high note.

Try the following, slowly, on open strings.

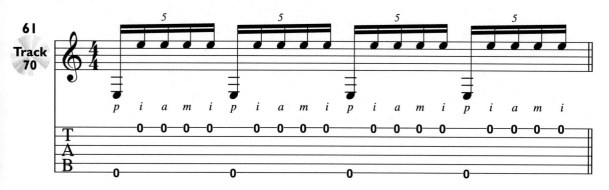

The following exercise will help you develop the necessary thumb mobility for playing tremolo. Throughout this exercise, keep your *i*, *m*, and *a* fingers on the 1st string to develop independence in the thumb.

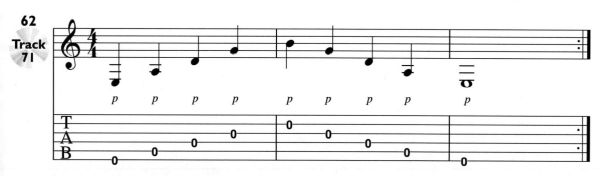

Now, combine the previous two examples and try the following.

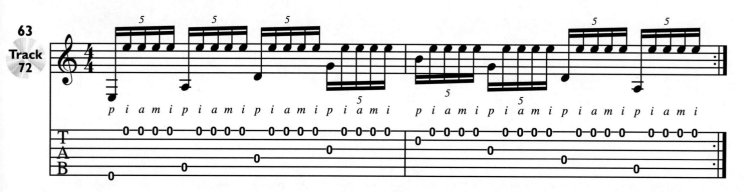

Add the exercise below to your daily routine. Here, we are applying the tremolo technique to a chord progression.

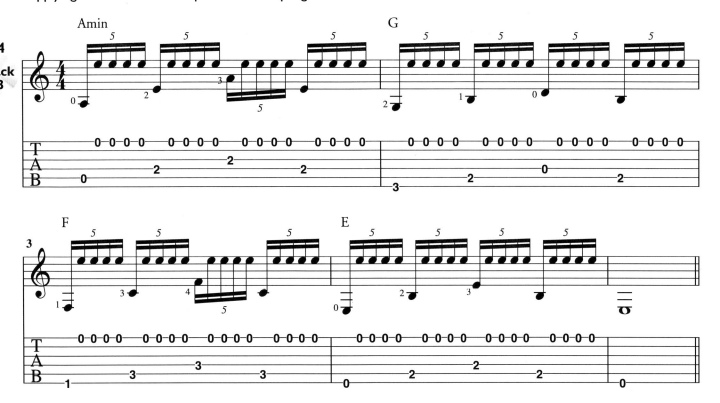

The Capo (Cejilla)

A capo is a device that is clamped onto the fretboard to raise the pitch of the strings. The use of the capo, or *cejilla* (pronounced *the-HE-ya* in Spanish), is very common in flamenco. Its most obvious application is during the accompaniment of singers, to adapt to their individual vocal ranges. It is also used frequently, however, for solo guitar pieces. At the beginning of a piece, an indication will be made as to what fret the capo should be placed (Capo II = 2nd fret, Capo III = 3rd fret, etc.).

The use of the cejilla for solo pieces can do several things. First, it tightens the strings so they don't move as much, which can help in faster moving tempos. Second, the tension this creates can help give a little more snap and punch to the guitar's sound. Third, it may make certain left-hand stretches more comfortable (because of the shorter distance between frets as you go up the guitar neck) and is a good tool when learning difficult left-hand passages that may ultimately be played without the cejilla. Fourth, it gives everything a different color, depending on where you place the cejilla; you may find you prefer the pitch and tone of certain pieces a little higher or lower on the fretboard. And with the cejilla, we can just change to another fret, or take it off entirely, to suit our mood or how the hand is feeling on a certain day.

Below are four types of cejillas commonly used in flamenco. The first (at far left) is the most traditional, and it is made of wood, leather, and a guitar string. All of these capos, however, are very effective.

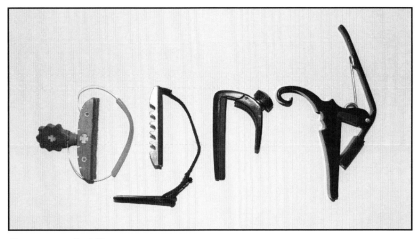

Four types of cejillas.

Barre Chords

To *barre* is to fret two or more strings with one finger. The finger must lie flat across the strings to accomplish a good, clean barre. In principle, the barre is simple, but it can be a source of tension and hand fatigue for many players.

When one finger barres all six strings, it is called a *full barre*. All other barres are called *partial barres*.

In chord diagrams, a barre is indicated by a curved line ⌒. Check out the diagram and photo below demonstrating an A Major full barre chord.

A Major (Full Barre Chord)

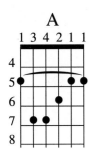
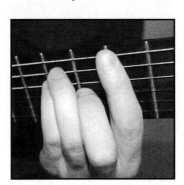

When playing barre chords, it is important to strive for a good, clean sound from each of the notes and to keep the hand free of tension. A few tips for developing this are as follows:

1. Practice placing your finger in the barre position but do not squeeze all the way. Make sure your other fingers are relaxed. Play around with this a little bit every day to familiarize your hand with this position. You may find that you start squeezing down the notes, naturally and easily, without even trying.

2. The position and movement of the left-hand thumb is very important. Keeping the thumb relatively low on the neck, it should remain straight—with a gentle squeeze coming from the thenar eminence (the large muscle in the palm that moves the thumb).

Proper thumb position for playing barre chords.

3. Partial barre chords are as common as full barre chords, so be sure to practice steps 1 and 2 using anywhere from two to five strings. Check out the picture of a partial barre below.

Partial barre.

For Practice

The following will help you develop good barring technique. Fret a note on the high-E string with your left-hand index finger, then pluck it with the right hand to make sure it produces a clean tone. Now, slide your left-hand fingertip up one string at a time—making a two-string bar, then a three-string barre, and so on. Each time you fret an additional string, pluck with your right hand to make sure each note sounds clean. Continue adding strings until you are fretting all six. Do this slowly enough so as not to increase tension. If you do feel tension, try starting with a single note and adding one string per day. This can save you from experiencing a lot of cramps and unnecessary tension.

In Written Music

In written music, a full barre is indicated as follows: CIII. The "C" indicates the barre and the Roman numeral indicates the fret at which the barre occurs. So, in the example given, a full barre is called for at the 3rd fret.

When you see 1/2 CV, you are being told to barre three strings at the 5th fret. When you see 2/3 CV, you are being told to barre four strings at the 5th fret.

Chapter 6: Progressive Solos

Like Chapter 4 (page 52), the material in this chapter incorporates and builds on all the previous lessons. The solo pieces in this chapter are "graded," progressing from relatively simple to early advanced. These pieces represent the palos you are most likely to need if you plan to perform as a flamenco guitarist.

In many of the pieces, there are markers (A, B, C, etc.) where something specific is pointed out that is necessary for the proper performance of that piece. The performance notes to which these markers correspond are listed before each piece (see below).

Fandangos de Huelva

Fandangos de Huelva are a large group of variations on the fandango style from the Andalucian province of Huelva. Most provinces in Andalucia have their own variations of the fandango, but Huelva is famous for its unusually large number of them.

Variation in the fandangos occurs primarily in the melody, rather than in the rhythm. Therefore, the guitarist's primary function is the same, regardless of which variety is being sung. That being said, there is no way around the deep and thorough listening you must do to familiarize yourself with the nuances in flamenco; this is absolutely necessary to become a capable and well-rounded accompanist.

This version of fandangos de Huelva—our first full-length solo piece—incorporates the signature cadential pattern of the fandangos and a very clear rendering of a traditional fandango *copla,* or verse. The form is also danced quite frequently and the version here can be used to play for dancers when there is no singer present. The dancer will likely request more than one copla, and until you acquire additional variations, this basic one can be repeated.

In this introductory solo piece, we have a chance to practice the rhythmic strumming pattern of the fandangos de Huelva, while simultaneously developing the essential skill of creating the dialogue between melody and accompaniment. Very often in solo playing, we simulate the singer and then create the accompaniment by strumming a chord in the spaces between the melodic phrases. By listening to flamenco singing, we develop the character of the flamenco voice (which we should strive to emulate in our melodic playing), while filling our ears with the subtleties of *cante* (see page 118) accompaniment.

Performance Notes

A First melodic phrase of the copla

B First chord in the accompaniment

C Let chords ring out as long as possible—in this case, leaving fingers 1, 2, and 3 holding the C chord, as you use the pinky and open strings to create the next melodic fragment

D Slight variation of chordal accompaniment

E End of copla

Fandangos de Huelva

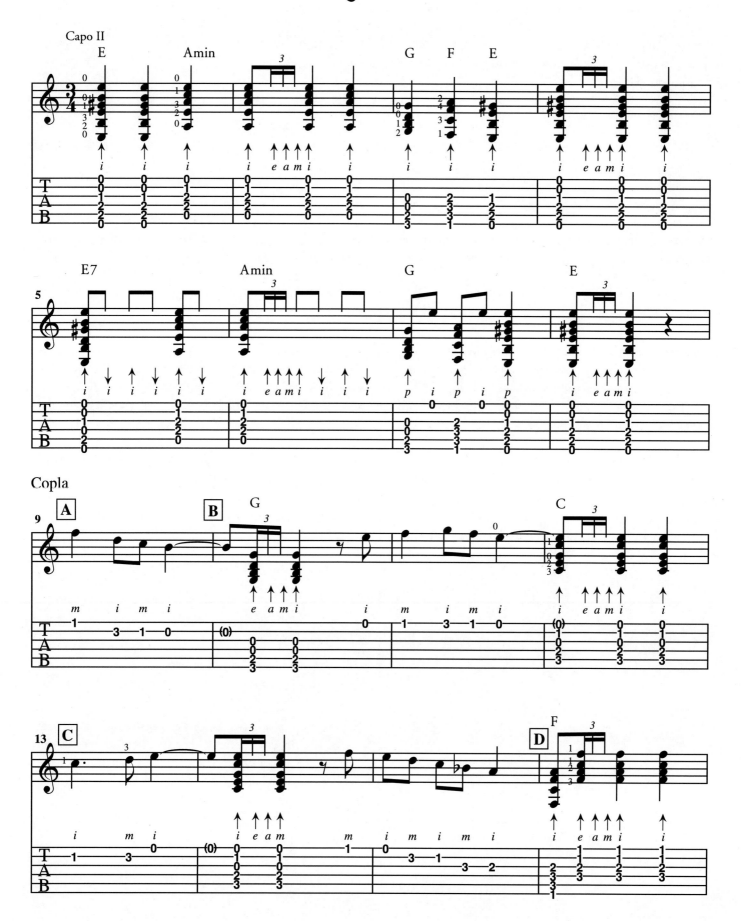

Rumba

The rumba comes to flamenco via the Cuban rumba form. Its catchy $\frac{4}{4}$ rhythm makes it one of the most popular of all flamenco styles—crossing over easily into commercial realms, as well as making it a favorite for parties and festive occasions. Rumbas are similar to the tangos but are generally faster and have more rhythmic emphasis on offbeats (see written example below).

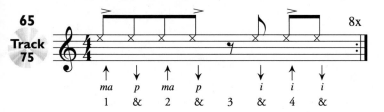

The rumba became popular in the late 1950s through the music of El Peret, a famous singer from Barcelona. The rumba is outside the range of some singers who may regard themselves as sticking to a purer version of flamenco. At the same time, however, the form has been embraced wholeheartedly by many within the flamenco tradition.

The following piece is intended to be played by two guitars—one playing the melody and the other (or others) playing the chordal accompaniment.

The chordal accompaniment has been provided on the accompanying CD (Track 78) so you can play the melody along with it. You will also want to play the chords along with the recording to develop your rumba rhythm skills. To play the rhythm part in this piece, you will need to learn several new chords; the diagrams for these are below.

This rumba is a great piece to improvise on. A typical format would be what jazz players refer to as "head in, solos, head out." The term *head* refers to the written melody. It would only be after the final time through melody, after the solos, that you would play all three endings. This approach has become very popular and is one of the most obvious ways in which we see a fusion of flamenco with other jazz and Latin styles.

Below is a basic approach for strumming in the rumba style.

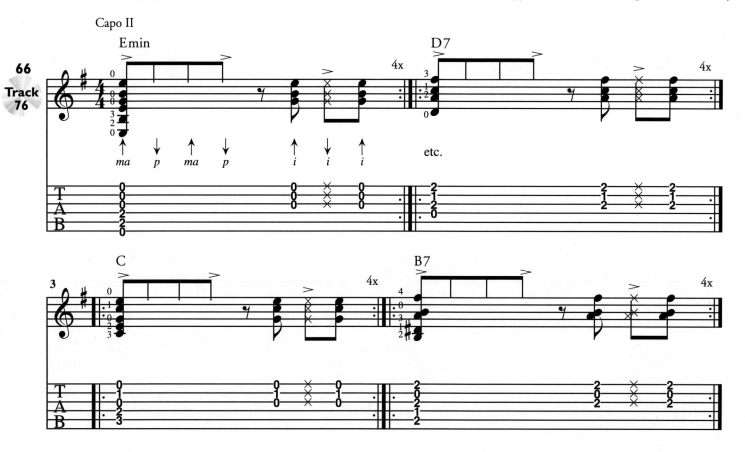

To the right are the new chords you will need to play the rhythm part for the following tune.

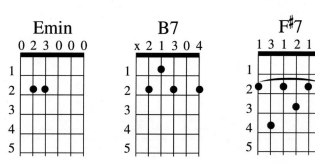

Rumba

Track 77 · *Chords and Melody*   Track 78 · *Chords*

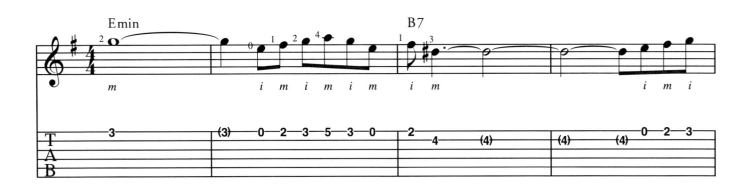

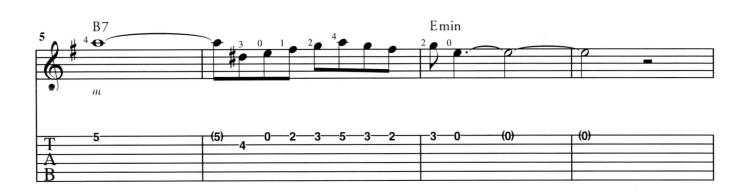

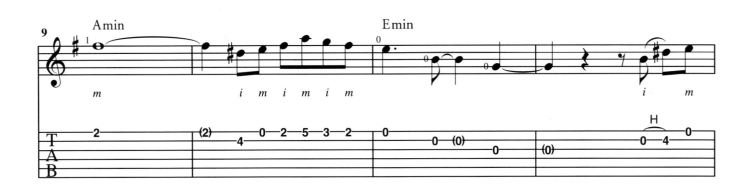

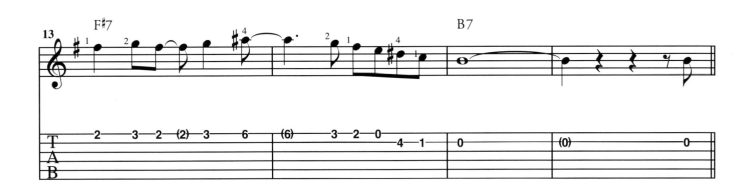

Continued on next page

Sevillanas

The sevillana is a form very much associated with flamenco, though not technically from the flamenco tradition. It is a Spanish folkloric song and dance, very popular not only in the city of Sevilla, for which the dance is named, but throughout all of Andalucia and Spain as a whole. It is one of the very festive forms in flamenco, and during the annual *ferias* (holidays) of southern Spain, sevillanas are danced to live—as well as recorded—music around the clock.

As a dance, it has a set structure and is most often danced in pairs—two elements in sharp contrast to the traditional flamenco aesthetic. Many flamenco artists don't regard sevillanas as flamenco, while many of the greatest flamenco artists have performed memorable, flamenco-ized versions of the style.

Sevillanas can be performed at a wide variety of tempos but are commonly done at fairly brisk speeds, especially when performed for an audience. The more flamenco-ized versions tend, however, to be much slower (check out flamenco singer Camarón de la Isla's version of "Sevillanas de Carlos Saura").

There are a few essential things to know about playing the sevillanas. As mentioned before, they have a strictly defined structure, being comprised of four equal portions, each of which is called a sevillana. In this book, we have three different sevillanas, each using a different key (which is quite common).

The combination of the sevillana's popularity with the defined meter and length make it a popular form for composers. You can do most anything harmonically or melodically to a sevillana—as long as the rhythm and starts and stops are right!

When danced or played as a solo, it is most common to play four sevillanas. Using the ones in this book, you may play the same sevillana for the first and fourth. You may also play any of them multiple times if you so choose. Again, what the dancers need is the clear rhythm and proper length. The choice of music can be up to you; you may want to experiment with changing the order and, eventually, substituting other sevillanas as your repertoire expands.

Following is the structure of the sevillana, the parts of which are indicated in "Sevillana No. 1" (next page).

1. Introduction of strummed chords, the length of this may vary

2. *Salida.* This is the opening phrase of the song, the very end of which is where the dancers begin

3. Rhythmic linking phrase consisting of nine beats (one and a half measures)

4. Melody—Four and a half measures long

   Then, play parts 3 and 4 two more times.

Sevillana No. 1

Sevillana No. 2

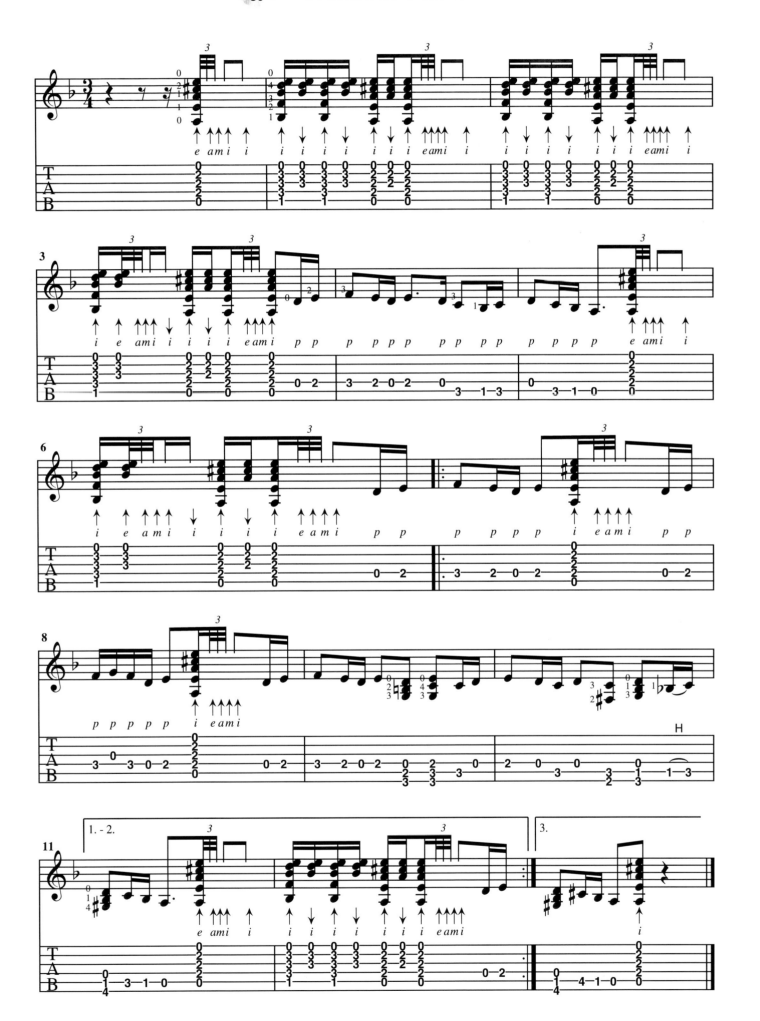

Sevillana No. 3

Alegrías

Alegrías, which means "happiness," or "joy," is one of the few forms in flamenco that uses a major key. It originates in the port city of *Cádiz* (pronounced CA-dees) and is said to have been influenced by northern Spanish song and dance forms. The people of Cádiz are famous for their humor and lively spirit, and the alegrías is one expression of that spirit.

The rhythmic backdrop of the alegrías is a very strong $\frac{3}{4}$ feel. However, in its modern form, it uses the same basic accent patterns as the other forms in the soleá family (see below).

12 | 1 2 **3** 4 5 **6** 7 **8** 9 **10** 11 (**12** 1 2 **3** etc.)

12 | 1 2 **3** 4 5 6 **7** **8** 9 **10** 11 (**12** 1 2 **3** etc.)

The alegrías is one of the most commonly chosen dances by dancers—having various sections, including a slower middle section that modulates to a minor key. This section is referred to as the *silencio* (meaning silence) and focuses on lyrical upper-body movement. This section typically has no footwork, in contrast to much of the rest of the dance. The music itself almost always ends in what is called *bulerías de Cádiz* and uses the rhythmic feel of the bulería while staying in the major tonality of the alegrías.

The piece on the next page gives a great sense of the spirit of the alegrías. The rhythmic sections provide an excellent opportunity to develop the *a-m-i-i* rasgueado and should, with time, feel very lively.

Performance Notes

A The transition from rasgueado to arpeggio is something to focus on. Between the two techniques, the fingers switch direction from outward to inward and therefore switch the muscle groups being used. For that reason, it is important to practice slowly, allowing the hand and forearm to fully relax before doing the arpeggio. We do not want to create tension by not fully letting go of the rasgueado.

B This little thumb falseta has a very traditional flavor and is in the style of the great flamenco guitarist Diego del Gastor (1908–1973).

Alegrías

Falseta

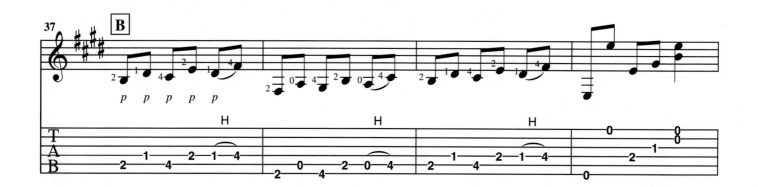

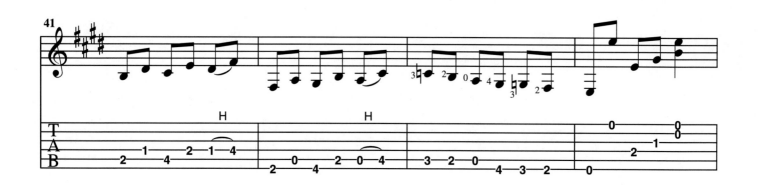

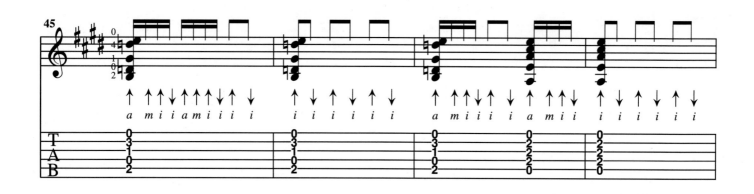

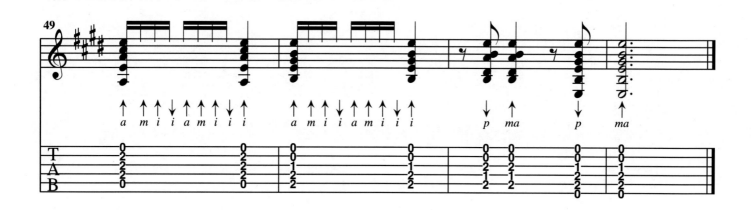

Tangos

As mentioned earlier in the book, the tangos is—along with the bulería and perhaps also the rumba—one of the most popular of all the cantes festeros (festive songs) in flamenco. In a robust $\frac{4}{4}$ rhythm, it shares the same name as the Argentinian tango, but is very much a separate form.

The tangos is one of the forms that is equally likely to appear in a cante recital, or recording, performed by a dancer or strictly as an instrumental. Because of its similarity to the rumba, it is often hard to distinguish one from the other, though the rumba is generally faster. It is not uncommon to see a recorded piece labeled as "tango rumba," and songs with this blend often have a pop or commercial dimension.

Performance Notes

A This tangos opens with a lengthy rhythmic section, first in tapada, then with chords. Work to develop comfort and rhythmic flow, then seek to have that same flow permeate the entire piece.

B Take advantage of the open A string to shift over to 3rd position, which begins immediately with the G note in the bass.

C Pay careful attention to the fingerings. The flow here comes from a fluid and consistent transition from thumb to fingers.

Alzapúa

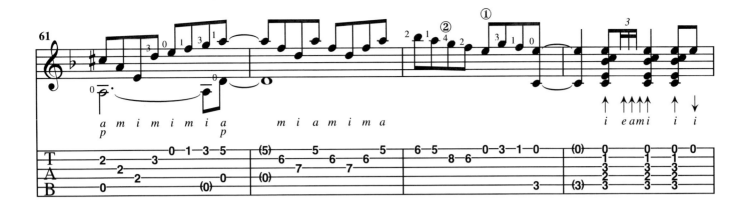

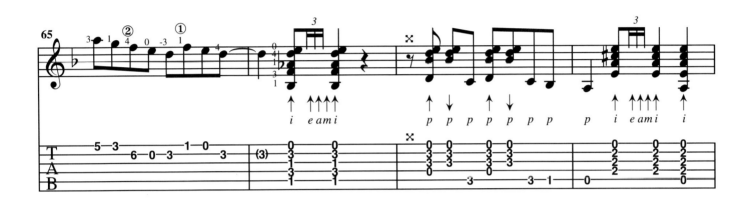

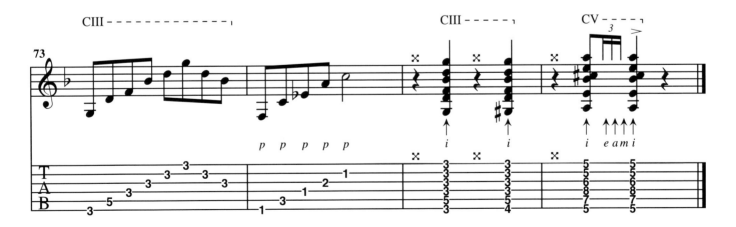

Siguiriyas

The siguiriyas is perhaps the most intense and emotional of all the flamenco palos. Like the soleá, it deals with themes of great loss and suffering, and when sung, obliges the singer to go deep within, pushing themselves to the limits of their vocal and expressive ability.

"Siguiriyas" is related the word "seguidilla," the name of another Spanish musical form—though, musically, there is no particular correlation. It is one of the palos that found its evolution in the flamenco triangle of Jerez, Cádiz, and Triana, and is regarded as one of the true gypsy forms of flamenco. Great singers of this form include Manuel Torre, Antonio Mairena, and El Terremoto de Jerez.

Performance Notes

A Continuous rasgueados of this sort are very common in siguiriyas. The slower tempo of the siguiriya makes it possible to practice these flourishes more easily than in some of the faster palos (where this type of technique may also be used).

B Here, we combine a downstroke played by the thumb with a golpe played by the ring finger. This combination is very common. As always, the best results come from keeping the hand totally relaxed.

C This triplet ornament should be practiced by itself. We hold the A Major chord with fingers 1 and 2 and perform the ornament with the 3rd finger. Practice at first by making the chord and moving the 3rd finger around in the air. You want to develop finger independence so that holding the chord has no effect on the 3rd finger. It is beneficial to develop some sense of freedom in the 3rd finger before trying to do the ornament, as performing it with a tense finger does not sound or feel good.

D This upstroke can be done with the thumb, as written, or with the *i* finger. It is a lighter stroke than the downstroke that precedes it and, with practice, should flow smoothly into the short thumb sequence that follows.

Siguiriyas

Capo III

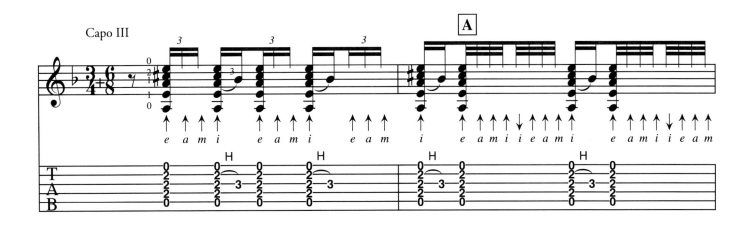

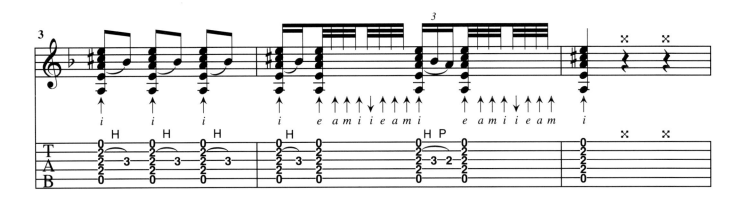

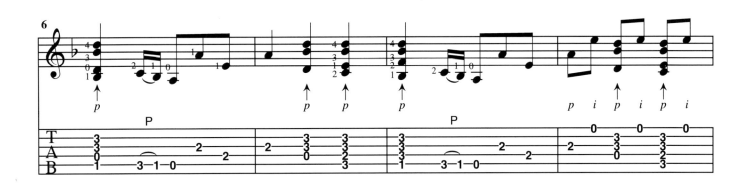

Falseta

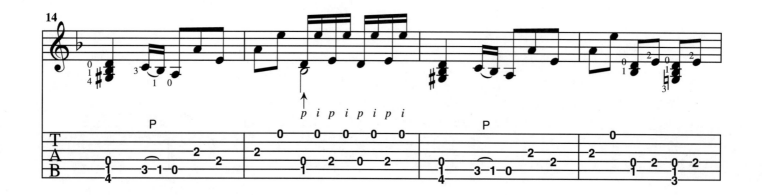

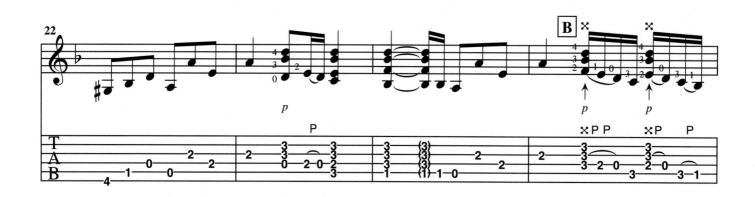

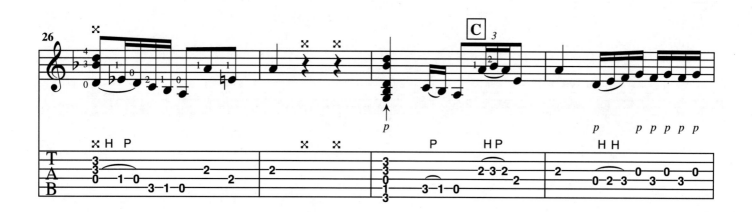

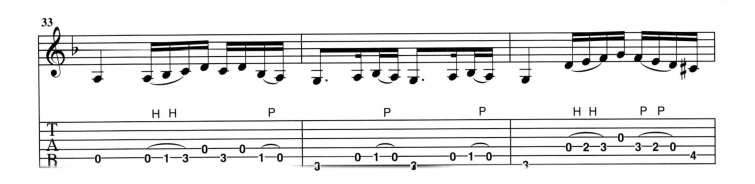

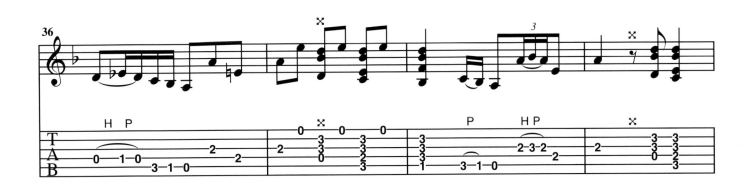

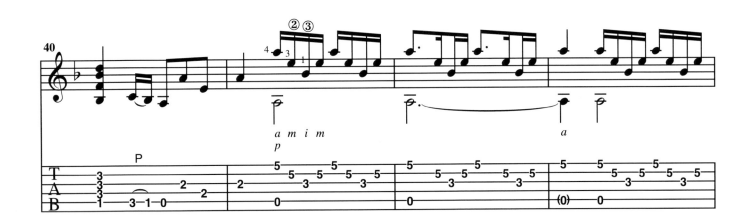

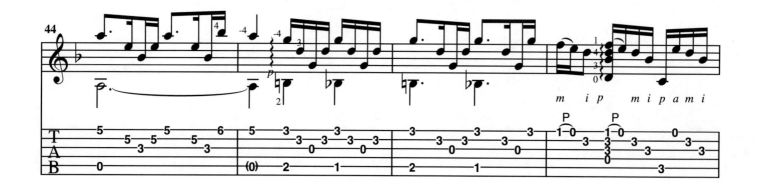

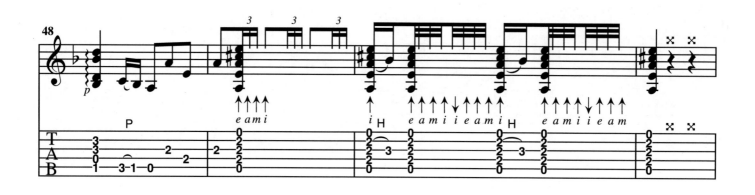

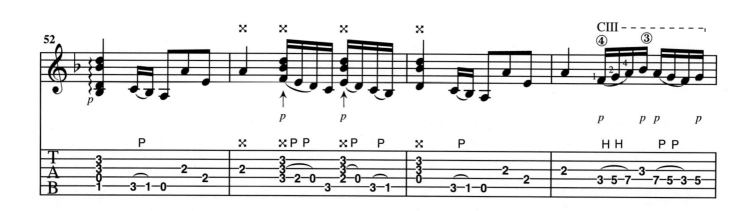

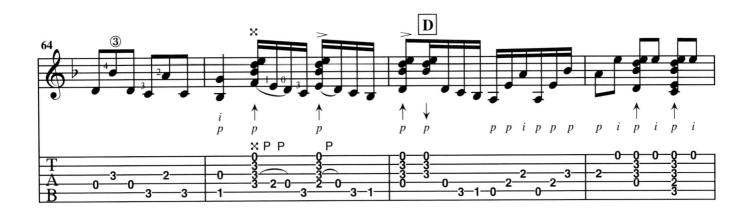

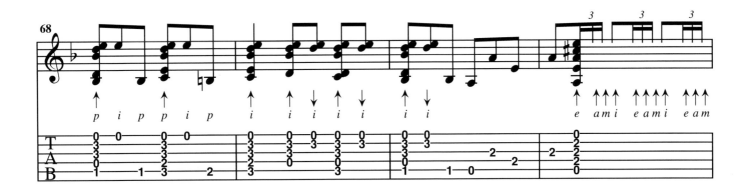

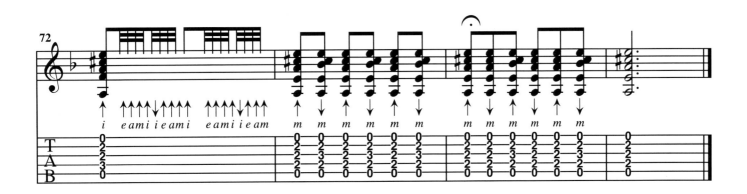

Bulerías

Bulerías is one of *the* most popular of all the flamenco palos. It originates from the city of Jerez de la Frontera, where many of the greatest singers, dancers, and guitarists in this palo were born, or have lived for a time. The word *"bulerías"* is said to come from "burlar," meaning to joke around, and bulerías is often sung in fiestas, where improvised lyrics and dance steps are contributed by everyone and are often intended to be quite funny or clever.

Because of its fast tempos and pulsing rhythms, the bulerías presents the opportunity for guitarists to show their rhythmic mastery and basic groove skills.

Performance Notes

This bulerías features a number of characteristic variations of the compás. Ultimately, these can be played in different orders, or if you are enjoying playing compás between falsetas, you may wish to play one or more additional compáses before going to the next falseta. This piece also develops picado and alzapúa, and ends with a flourish of the abanico rasgueado.

The last chord in this piece ends with a variation on the A Major chord (technically an A7) that is very popular in bulerías and tangos. The G note is played on the 6th string, and the notes on the 2nd fret of the 2nd, 3rd, and 4th strings are barred with the 1st finger. If this chord is difficult at first, you can substitute a regular A Major chord.

Another Voicing for the A Chord

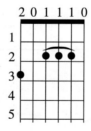

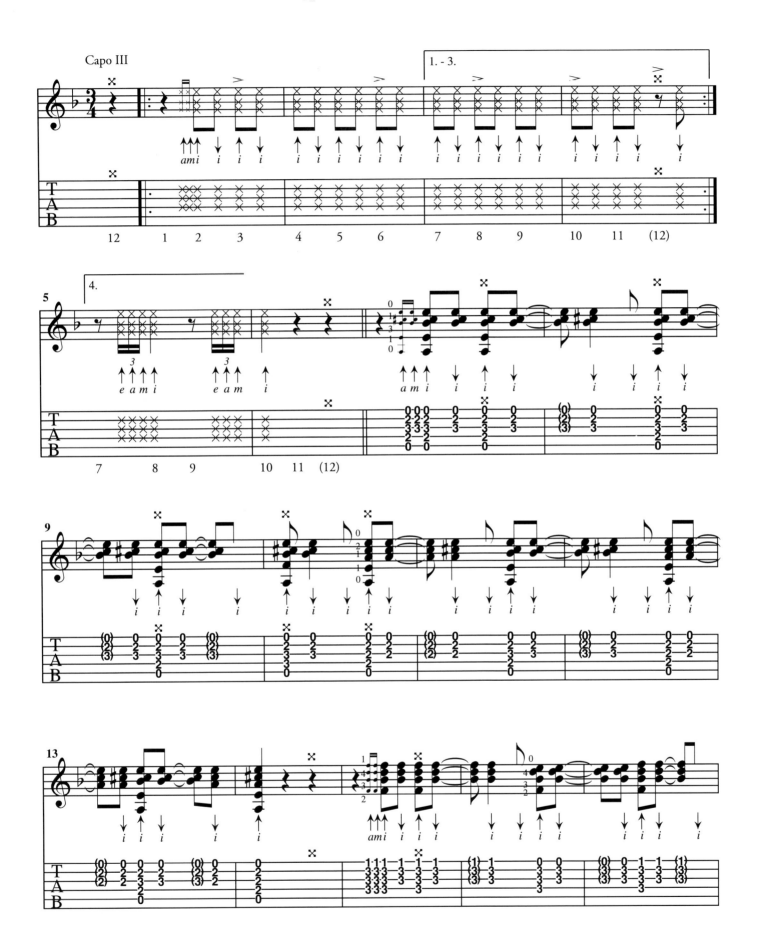

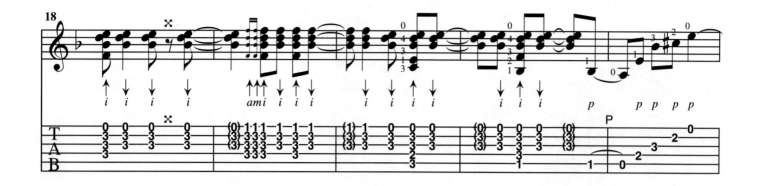

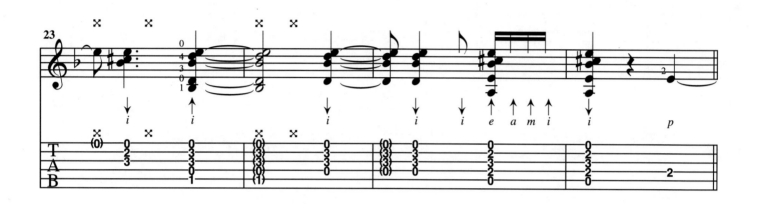

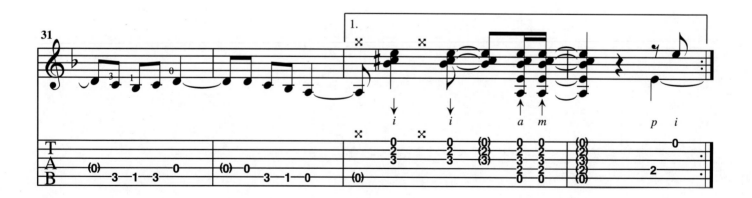

Soleá

The soleá is regarded as one of the most ancient of all flamenco song forms. The siguiriya and soleá form the heart of the cante jondo tradition, and when sung, typically deal with themes of sadness (e.g., lost love, a departed family member, etc.), and even themes of vengeance or betrayal.

The word "soleá," or "soleares" as it is also called, comes from the Spanish word "soledad" (solitude). The serious and passionate expression of the soleá is, therefore, a deeply personal expression of some form of pain or longing.

On the guitar, the soleá is generally played in the "key" of E Phrygian, though it can also be found in A Phrygian (the key most often used for a close relative called soleá por bulerías—a form of bulerías that borrows the soleá compás).

There is a lot of space in the soleá, and also something called peso (weight) in the beats, to clearly mark the slow but deliberate rhythm of this palo.

Performance Notes

A This piece starts by playing around the E chord in the 7th position, a frequently used alternative to the open E chord.

B This is a two-string alzapúa.

C This falseta is among the most traditional soleá falsetas.

D This falseta is a variation on another traditional falseta. Pay special attention to the correct right- and left-hand fingerings for the arpeggios on the upper strings.

E The melody in the tremolo section is fairly active. This may require a fair amount of slow practice to execute comfortably and smoothly. Take frequent breaks if you feel your left hand getting sore or tight. Tremolo on the 2nd string (measures 69 and 73) will also require extra practice. Practice slowly enough to hear each note clearly and separately before speeding up.

F This is a four-stroke rasgueado, though you could also choose to use five strokes.

G Here, we use the index finger rather than the thumb on the last note of the scale. The use of i and m all the way through the 6th string is very important for the even flow of the scale. The following m finger on the high E is not as tricky as it might seem. Practice slowly, and if needed, you may at first want to skip the high-E note altogether; it is essentially an ornament and should not be a source of undue struggle.

Soleá

Track 86

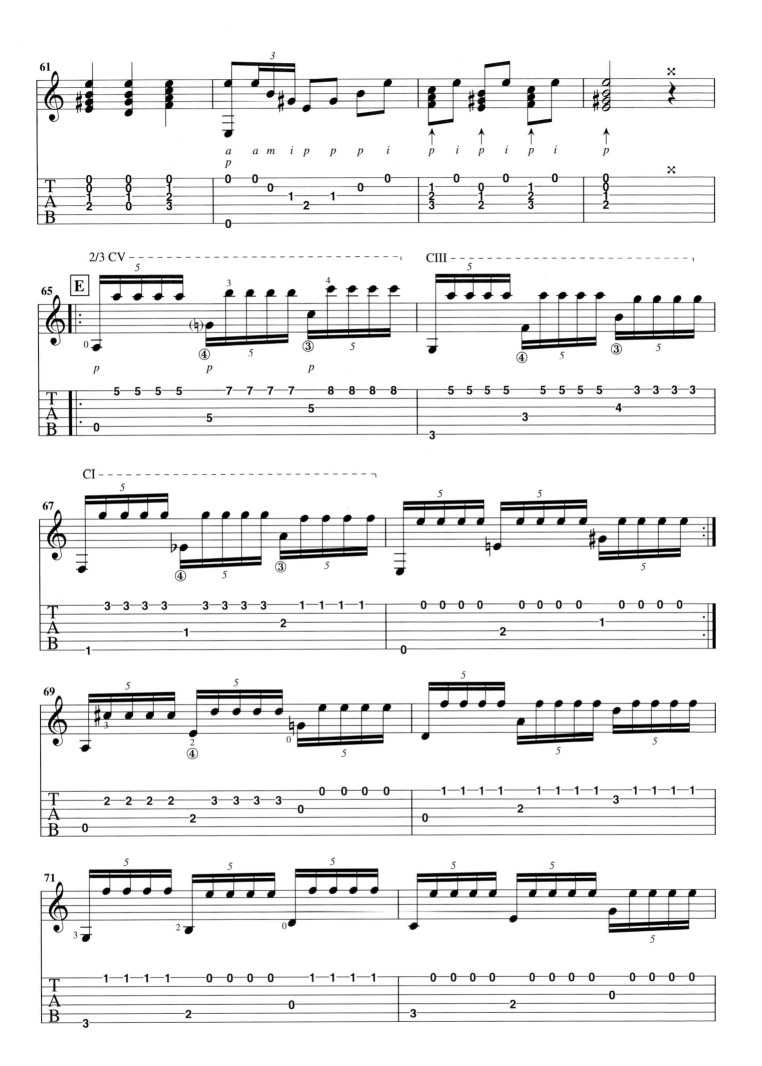

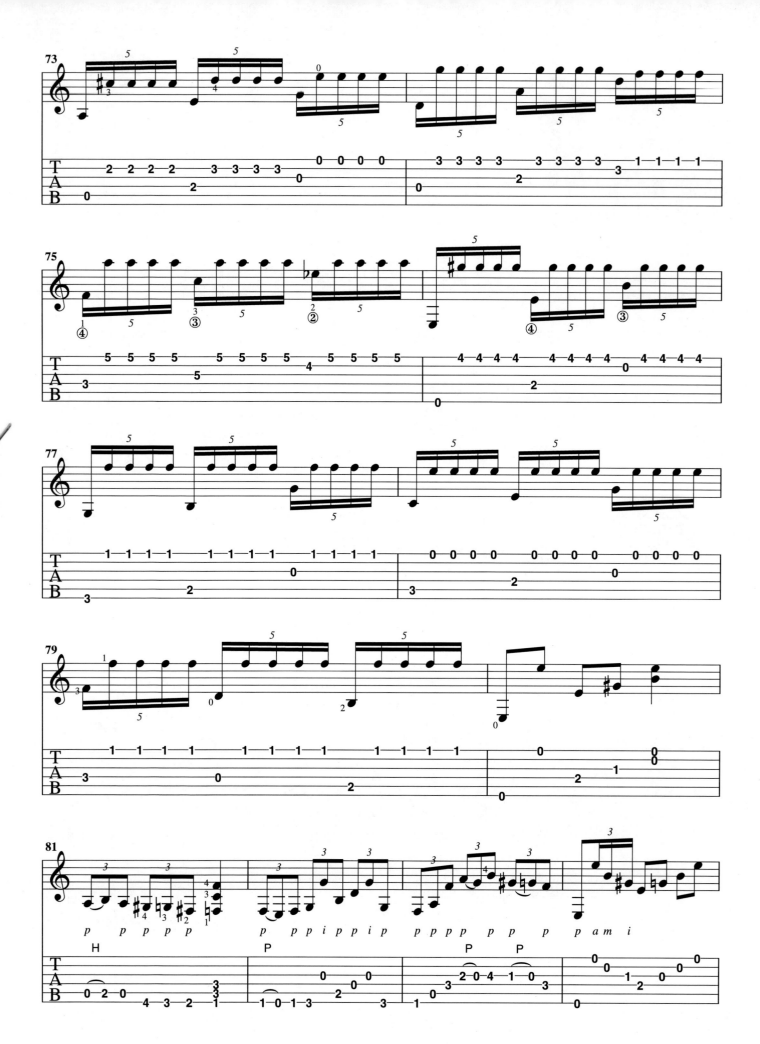

Farruca

The farruca is one of the only forms in all of flamenco that is primarily associated with dance and guitar. A popular dance throughout Spain at the beginning of the 20th century, it adapted tangos movements to the music of the farruca. Originally danced by men, the legendary Carmen Amaya broke the gender barrier in the 1930s by putting on pants and dancing farruca with her extraordinary footwork.

The farruca's $\frac{4}{4}$ rhythm and characteristic minor key distinguish it from other flamenco forms, as the vast majority of them use either Phrygian or major tonalities.

The great guitarist Sabicas recorded many versions of the farruca and his influence is apparent in parts of this composition.

Performance Notes

[A] The opening chord sequence is Amin to F (really, F Major 7th). Keep the fingers in the Amin position, playing the G note in the bass with the pinky, and only moving the 1st finger to play the F note (leaving the other fingers in place).

[B] Here, we switch from index finger to thumb. Watch the right-hand fingerings carefully.

[C] Once again, we keep the Amin chord position while only the left-hand pinky moves to finger the different bass notes.

[D] Here, we are arpeggiating with the thumb. Finger each of these groups of four notes as a single chord (F, E7, then Amin) in the left hand, letting them ring out until you need to switch to the next chord.

Farruca

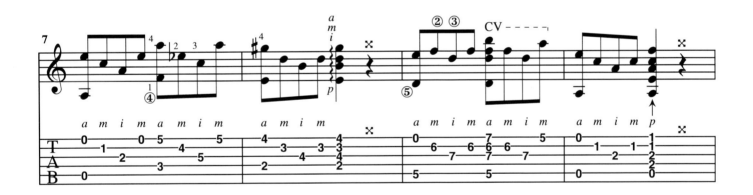

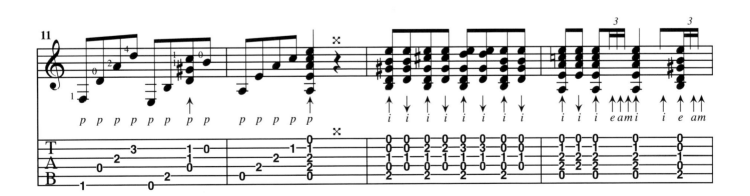

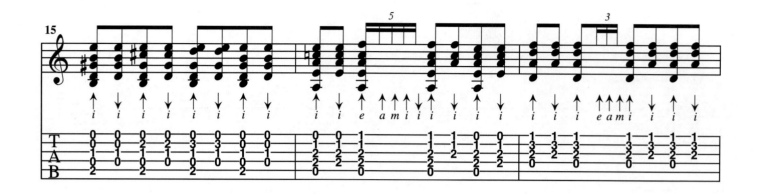

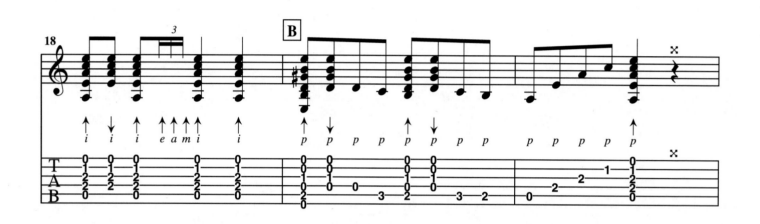

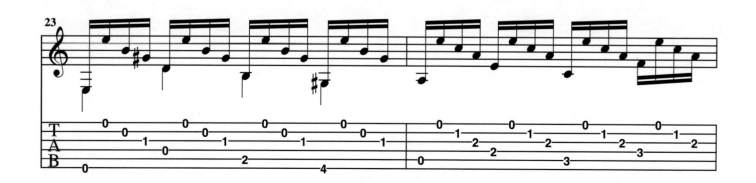

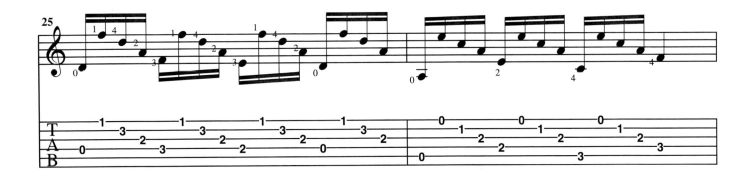

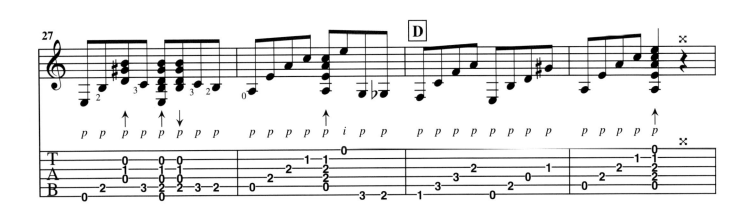

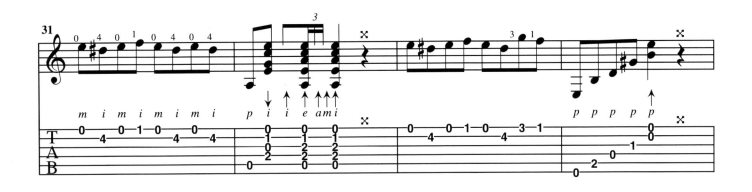

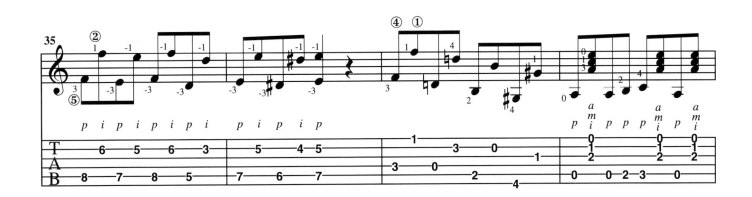

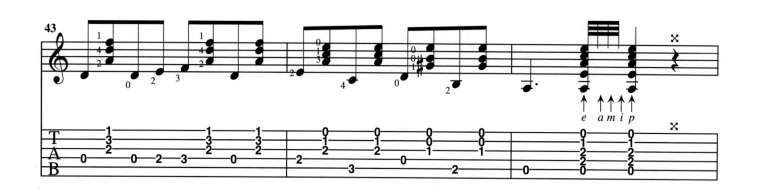

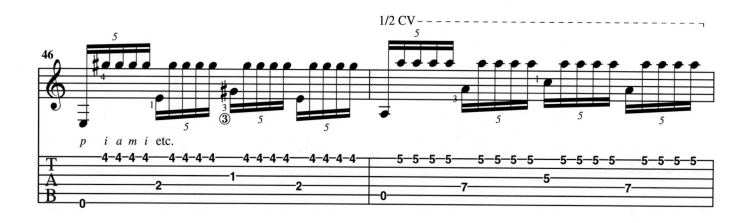

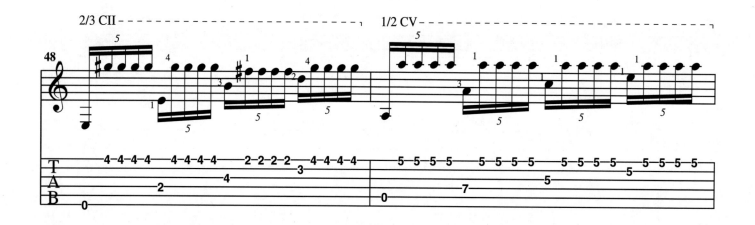

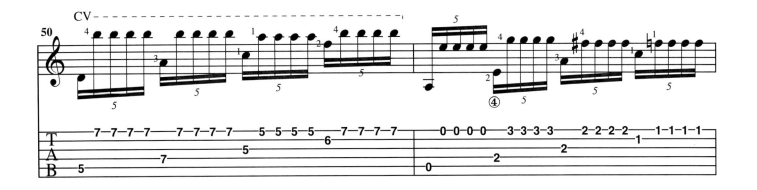

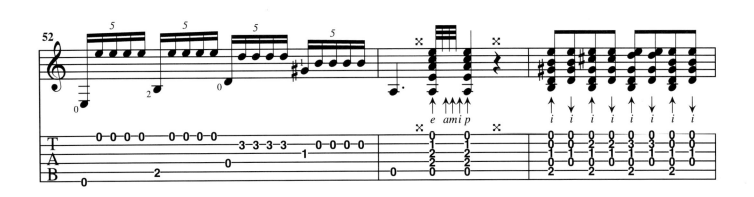

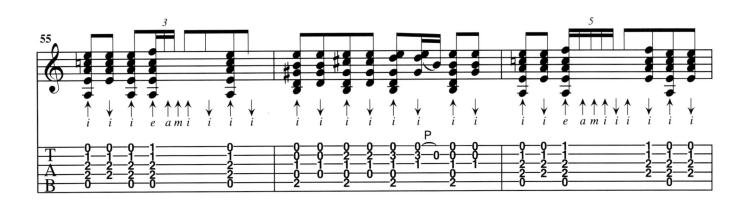

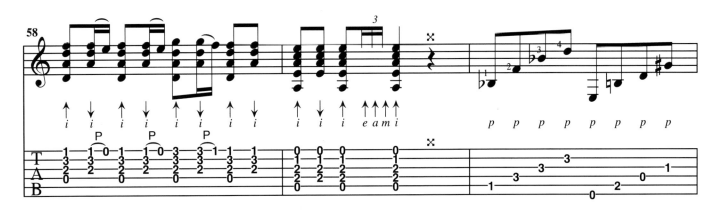

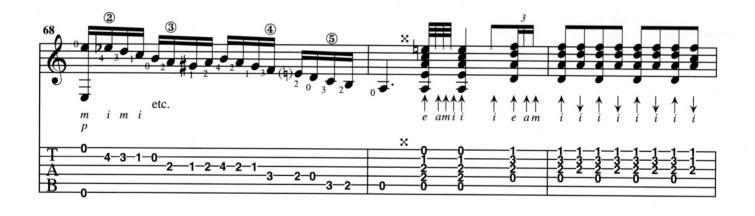

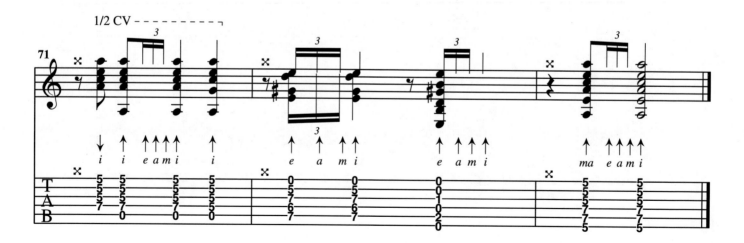

Conclusion

Congratulations on finishing *The Total Flamenco Guitarist!* Flamenco is a thriving and evolving art form—one that, with patience and consistent practice, we can enjoy for a lifetime. We hope this book has provided valuable guidance and an enjoyable challenge with rewarding results. We also hope you will continue to explore the depth and breadth of this multifaceted art form through listening, viewing videos, and reading—but especially through spending time around and participating in live flamenco (preferably in Spain if you have the opportunity!). Music of any style, and flamenco for certain, can provide an endless source of challenge and reward. Whether you have just taken a few ideas, or are practicing material from this book several hours a day and are hungry for more, it is hoped that this book plays a useful and enjoyable role in your process.

In closing, music is much like life, in that we can keep evolving if we set our mind to it. To evolve as guitarists, we need to listen, observe, practice, play, and enjoy!

PHOTO BY MONTUNO

Paco de Lucía (born Francisco Sánchez Gómez in 1947) is without a doubt the most influential figure in flamenco guitar since the last third of the 20th century. The youngest in a family of flamenco guitarists and singers, he was a child prodigy who first toured America at age 14. His early recordings demonstrate a mastery of traditional forms, both as a soloist and accompanist. His numerous collaborations with jazz, classical, and assorted world music artists led Paco to revolutionize the language of flamenco, greatly expanding the tradition through jazz harmonies and improvisation, and the incorporation of non-traditional instruments, including electric bass and drumset.

Appendix A: Glossary of Flamenco Terms

Note: Not all of the following terms are used in this book, but they will be useful as you continue your flamenco studies.

Aire—Literally means "air" and refers to the flavor, or character, of a particular form (as in the "aire of alegrías"). It also refers to the more general idea of playing with musicality and feel (as in "having a lot of aire").

Baile—Dance. One of the key elements in flamenco.

Cajón—Percussion instrument that resembles a box. Originally used in various styles of Latin American music, the cajón became a staple of flamenco music starting in the early 1980s when Paco de Lucia's percussionist Rubem Dantas began using it regularly with the group. It caught on quickly because its sounds blend naturally with the crisp, percussive snap of the palmas, heelwork, and guitar strums.

Cante—Flamenco singing, or cante flamenco. The original and primary component of flamenco, generally divided into the following two categories.

Cante jondo—Means "deep song" and refers to songs in the palos of soleá, siguiriyas, martinetes, etc. that share the qualities of slow and very profound emotional expression. Cante jondo lyrics often deal with themes of loss, death, broken-heartedness, and other daily struggles.

Cante chico—Means "little song" and refers to the much lighter festive forms including bulerías, rumba, tangos, etc.

Cantes libres—Means "free songs." Cantes libres is an important group of songs in the flamenco repertoire. As guitar solos, they are referred to as *toques libres* (*toque* is derived from the Spanish verb *tocar,* or "to play an instrument"). Songs in this group have no strict rhythmic meter; they are performed in a free-flowing way with pauses and flourishes that allow the singer or guitarist to express a great deal of emotion. The forms that fit under this heading include the tarantas, mineras, cartageneras, granaína, fandangos libres, malagueñas, and, on the guitar, the rondeña (not the sung form, which uses a three-beat compás). For the purposes of this book, we have focused on the rhythmic palos, as all of the same techniques used in the free forms are the same as those used in rhythmic forms. Additionally, a solid grounding in the rhythmic forms is essential to achieve the internal pulse necessary for playing free songs.

Cejilla—Capo. A clamp-like device that is placed on the neck of the guitar to raise the pitch of the strings. In flamenco, the cejilla is used almost always when accompanying singers, to accommodate the singer's natural vocal range (though it is frequently used when playing solo guitar as well). The cejilla reduces the amplitude of the strings making their response a bit more immediate, as well as brightening up the tone and helping the projection of the instrument.

Compás—Rhythm. Compás refers to the specific rhythmic pattern of a given form, as in the twelve-beat pattern of alegrías. It is equivalent to the musical term "measure" in flamenco, as in "one measure of music." Compás also refers to the musicality, or "groove," as in having "good compás" (as is ascribed to many accomplished performers).

Contratiempo—Countertime. Refers to the placement of a sound—usually footwork of a dancer or the continuous on and offbeat interplay between two or more people doing palmas—that is so characteristic in flamenco. Especially in faster or more intense sections of a performance, the use of contratiempo in the palmas adds a great amount of energy and power to the overall experience.

Duende—Literally means "spirit" or "fairy-like creature." In flamenco, this term refers to the mysterious or magical quality that sometimes comes and then vanishes spontaneously in special moments of formal or informal music-making. This experience is often felt by everyone in attendance—whether a small gathering of friends and family, or in a larger performance setting. For many, *duende* is what flamenco is all about, a magical soul-stirring experience. For further insight into this concept, read Garcia Lorca's famous lecture *Teoría y Juego del Duende*.

Falseta—The brief melodic solos a guitarist plays as an introduction and/or interlude between verses when playing with singers and dancers. A well-rounded guitarist will have at least a handful of falsetas ready to go in any given palo and should eventually learn falsetas in all the *palos*. Importantly, falsetas also form the basis of a player's solo repertoire, as, indeed, a traditional guitar solo is simply an appealing sequence of selected falsetas from one's repertoire.

Guitarra—Guitar.

Jaleo—Shouts of encouragement given from a viewer or performer to another performer. This is an extremely important contribution to the overall emotion of a flamenco performance. Some common jaleos are words like "Ole!" or "Bien!"

Juerga—A party, usually spontaneous, where music and dancing take place. This is often considered the real learning ground, where one gets to try out and refine what they've practiced.

Llamada (pronounced ya-MA-da)—Means "call" and refers to the rhythmic phrase that exists in the different forms to let everyone know that a change is coming. It could "call" to the singer to begin, or it can let everyone know that a stop is coming up. Sometimes the llamada comes from the guitar and sometimes from the dancer; it is also part of the end of verses sung by singers. Llamadas are an integral part of the musical language of flamenco—a musical cue that keeps everyone together and creates a natural flow from one section to the next.

Palmas—The rhythmic hand-clapping that is so essential to flamenco. The two major types are palmas claras and palmas sordas.

Palmas Claras—"Clear" palmas used in louder and more intense moments, created by the fingers striking the open palm of the opposite hand.

Palmas Sordas—"Deaf" palmas used for softer sections and made by clapping the palm of one hand against the opposite palm. It creates a fleshier and more subdued sound than the clara.

Remate (pronounced re-MA-te)—Means "re-kill." A very important concept in flamenco having to do with creating a very decisive ending, in particular to falsetas. A great falseta with an unconvincing *remate* (finish) leaves everyone dissatisfied, while a simple or weakly played falseta with a powerful *remate* can get a heartfelt "Ole!" from a listener.

Soniquete—A term used to imply rhythmic feel, vitality, or groove—similar to when something "really swings" in jazz. Soniquete occurs once the basic rhythms are internalized enough to play at the next level, where the music really comes to life and makes everyone feel like dancing. This quality and/or ability is best developed by listening and seeing great performers, and by dancing and allowing your whole body to incorporate the nuances of the different rhythmic feels. Generally speaking, the great players of today are all regarded as having great soniquete, and this is a quality that can exist wherever there is rhythm (i.e., palmas, cajón, dancing, etc.).

Appendix B: Map of Spain

Below is a map of Spain and its surrounding areas.

Appendix C: Major Flamenco Guitarists

The following in no way represents a complete list of the many gifted and influential guitarists in flamenco; rather, it highlights a number of important guitarists that have shaped and/or continue to shape the evolution of the style. Listen to and enjoy all of these wonderful players and find the ones that speak to you. This is an essential part of learning the language and developing one's own style.

Without a doubt, development of the flamenco guitar as a solo instrument starts with Ramón Montoya and is followed by Niño Ricardo, Sabicas, Paco de Lucía, and Manolo Sanlúcar.

Other important guitarists from the first half of the 20th century include:

- El Habichuela
- Miguel Borrul
- Manolo de Huelva
- Melchor de Marchena
- Mario Escudero
- Diego del Gastor

In the second half of the 20th century, many great players emerged, including:

- Parrilla de Jerez
- Pepe Martinez
- Serranito
- Pedro Becán
- Manuel Morao
- Juan Habichuela
- Enrique Melchor
- Pepe Habichuela
- Paco del Gastor
- Niño Miguel
- Moraíto Chico
- Andrés Batista
- Juan Maya "Marote"

The modern, post–Paco de Lucía era has seen a large number of great players emerge, notably:

- Tomatito
- Vicente Amigo
- Gerardo Nuñez
- Rafael Riqueni
- Paco Jarana
- Juan Manuel Cañizares
- José Antonio Rodriguez
- Jerónimo Maya
- Montoyita
- Chuscales
- Carlos Heredia
- Antón Jiménez
- Jesús Losada "Jesules"
- Niño Josele
- Adam del Monte
- Canito
- Diego de Morao
- El Viejín
- Jesús de Rosario
- Paquete
- Paco Cortés
- Miguel Angel Cortés
- Pedro Cortes

Each of the players above is a master in their own right. When you listen to them, you will hear a great diversity in tone, chords, rhythmic feel, and attack. This diversity and individuality is fundamental to flamenco. The development and celebration of one's unique voice is something we too can strive for as we absorb the influences of these maestros and create our own musical path.

Appendix D: Geographical "Schools" of Flamenco Guitar

Over time, significant stylistic differences have evolved from one part of Andalucia to another. This is true even to the extent that you frequently hear differences from one town to the next—and even amongst different neighborhoods within the same town, such as Jerez's two famous Gypsy barrios, San Miguel and Santiago. These differences can include the typical speed at which a certain form is played, certain characteristic ways of accentuating a rhythm, relative looseness or tightness of the body in the dancing, and so on. Generally, each town considers its way to be the right way; though, interestingly, Jerez is universally considered to be a benchmark in the bulerías, as well as in the cante jondo—even by those who come from different "schools."

Following is a basic outline of the major schools of guitar, and a few of the major artists of each style.

Jerez
- Parilla de Jerez
- Manuel Morao
- Paco Cepero
- Antonio Jero
- Niño Jero
- Moraíto Chico

Morón de la Frontera/Lebríja
- Diego del Gastor
- Paco del Gastor
- Juan del Gastor
- David Serva
- Pedro Bacán
- Paco Fernandez
- Antonio Moya
- Martín Chico

Granada
- El Habichuela
- Juan Habichuela
- Pepe Habichuela
- Juan Maya "Marote"

Madrid/Caño Roto
- El Viejín
- El Entri
- Juan Ramón Jiménez
- El Morata
- Antón Jiménez
- Jerónimo Maya
- Jesús Losada "Jesules"

While there are any number of great and influential guitar players throughout Andalucia and other parts of Spain (Málaga, Sevilla, Córdoba, Almería, Barcelona, etc.), the regional schools listed above continue to have major influence and retain an identity while flamenco as a whole evolves and incorporates new influences. This does not negate the influence that people like Niño Ricardo and Paco de Lucía have had on the genre as a whole. Their influences have transcended region, thanks to recordings, television, and the Internet—which some purists feel is to the detriment of the local traditional styles. The Madrid group above does not have as long a history as the other places, and, indeed, the style there could be defined as a post–Paco de Lucía school, heavily influenced by the technical virtuosity and harmonic expansion that Paco brought to the art form.

Appendix E: Major Flamenco Singers

It is essential for a flamenco guitarist to be thoroughly versed in singing. For many, this can be an acquired taste, but singing was—and is—at the core of flamenco culture. In-depth familiarity with singing is not only essential if one hopes to be even a reasonable accompanist, but it is also the source of the emotional and expressive nature of flamenco. Paco de Lucía often mentions that he wished he was a singer and that what he strives for when he plays is to imitate a singer. This has a lot to do with the emotional impact and clarity he has always transmitted as a player. Also, much of the great guitar playing to be heard in flamenco is in this accompaniment setting. Not only are great falsetas to be heard throughout recordings and performances, but the art of how to create and sustain musicality and rhythm using all of the different techniques is best observed in this setting.

Following is a list of some of the greatest flamenco singers, past and present.

- Manuel Torre
- Tomás Pavón
- Patora Pavón
- Juanito Valderrama
- Porrinas de Badajóz
- Antonio Mairena
- Manolo Caracol
- El Agujetas
- El Chocolate

- Fernanda de Utrera
- Bernarda de Utrera
- Terremoto de Jerez
- La Perla de Cádiz
- Paco Toronjo
- Fosforito
- El Lebrijano
- Juanito Villar
- La Macanita

All of the above represent the more traditional side of *cante flamenco*.

The following singers come from a very traditional foundation and have explored some newer approaches as well.

- José Mercé

- Esperanza Fernandez

- La Macanita

- La Familia Montoya

- Enrique Morente

- Carmen Linares

The single biggest thing to happen to flamenco singing since 1970, however, was the appearance of Camarón de la Isla. He died in 1992 at the age of 41, but not before leaving a legacy of 17 recordings, 13 of which were with Paco de Lucía. He set a standard of expression and innovation that has sparked a whole generation of young singers, all cast in his mold to one degree or another. All of his recordings come highly recommended.

Below is a list of several of the top post-Camarón-era singers.

- Dieguito "El Cigala"

- El Potito

- Remedios Amaya

- El Duquende

- Montse Cortés

- Niña Pastori

- Estrella Morente

Appendix F: Major Flamenco Dancers

Dance Accompaniment

As mentioned in the beginning of this book, a "total flamenco guitarist" has knowledge and appreciation of all facets of flamenco, in other words, of cante and baile as well as guitarra. As with the accompaniment of singing, a great deal of the finest playing can be heard in dance accompaniment. In fact, many right-hand flamenco techniques were developed because of the need to support and emphasize—with the sound of the guitar—the dancer's different rhythms and body movements. That is to say, a lot of what we do as flamenco guitarists evolved from finding ways to create, with our fingers, the same rhythms the dancer makes with their feet.

Great dance accompaniment is a major discipline in flamenco; it is something that any serious flamenco player should incorporate to help solidify the various techniques and rhythms—even if this does not become a primary focus. As with the accompaniment of singing, virtually all of the great soloists have some significant experience with dance accompaniment. In the past, due to the demanding nature of dance accompaniment (the expectation of a certain intensity/volume), the players who emerged as outstanding soloists tended to drift away from this discipline, as it tends to take away from the subtlety and precision of some of the movements required for solo playing. This, however, has changed greatly since the 1980s, as microphones have come into nearly universal use. This has enabled a whole new era in dance accompaniment, where entire pieces—even whole performances—can be choreographed to intricately composed music, creating in some cases, note-for-note accompaniment of each movement done by the dancer. In the past, the vast majority of dance accompaniment consisted of powerful, usually unamplified strumming. Today, there is a mixture of this highly arranged, intricate accompaniment interspersed with the ever-indispensable strumming (now more likely to be reserved for punctuation and moments of peak intensity).

There are many great dancers throughout the history of flamenco, and many singers and guitarists are known for being excellent dancers as well. It is quite normal at the end of a performance for some of the musicians to take turns dancing, often to very enthusiastic applause.

Below is a list of some of the great dancers of the 20th and 21st centuries.

- Vicente Escudero
- Carmen Amaya
- Antonio el Bailaor
- El Farruco
- Miguel Funi
- Ciro
- El Güito
- Manolete
- Matilde Coral
- Manolo Marín
- Mario Maya
- Antonio Gades
- Cristina Hoyos
- Carmen Cortés
- Manuela Carrasco

- Juana Amaya
- Eva "La Yerbabuena"
- María Pagés
- Farruquito
- Farru
- Joaquín Cortés
- Domingo Ortega
- Juan Ramírez
- Joaquíín Grilo
- Alejandro Granados
- Sara Baras
- Isaac de los Reyes
- Nino de los Reyes
- Rocio Molina

Appendix G: Flamenco Percussion

While flamenco is a highly percussive music and dance, traditionally, the use of percussion has been fairly limited to the palmas, *pitos* (fingersnaps), *nudillos* (rapping knuckles on a tabletop or bar), and perhaps a *bastón* (cane) to tap out the rhythms on the floor.

It has only been since the 1970s that other percussion instruments have been incorporated into flamenco.

Instruments such as bongos, congas, shakers, and even drumset were already being used in the early 1980s, when Rubem Dantas (of Paco de Lucía's sextet) introduced the cajón. The use of this box-shaped percussion instrument caught on like wildfire and is now a staple of the genre. Other instruments have gained popularity in recent years, including clay drums like the udu, various frame drums, the African djembe, and even the Indian tabla.

Following are some of the most noted flamenco percussionists.

- Rubem Dantas

- Tino di Geraldo

- Ramón Porrina

- Piraña

- El Bandolero

- Sergio Martinez

- Nacho Arimany

- Diego Álvarez "El Negro"

Appendix H: Additional Resources on the Internet

The Internet has made flamenco available to the whole world, to an extent that far exceeds any previous era. For most of the art form's history, to experience live flamenco one either had to be in the right part of Spain at the right time or hope to catch an occasional traveling group. Finding recordings and/or books could also be a daunting task. For a long time and with few exceptions (major metropolitan cities like Paris and New York), the outlook was fairly bleak for the flamenco lover living outside of Spain. Now, there are virtually endless videos and recordings through a wide array of sources, notably YouTube.com. Most of the artists named in Appendices C–F can be found through a search on YouTube. Additionally, most of the contemporary artists have their own websites as well and may be available on other social networking sites such as MySpace.com. The existence of audio recordings, video recordings, and printed materials is at unprecedented levels and with unprecedented availability. All of this creates a rich pool of resources to learn from in a way that just simply was not possible until the 21st century. Still, there is little substitute for actually spending time in Spain, or in the presence of accomplished artists. In lieu of that, below is a list of websites that have information and access to recordings, instruments, and other products.

- www.youtube.com

- www.flamenco-connection.com

- www.flamencoworld.com

- www.esflamenco.com

- www.andalucia.org

- www.luthiermusic.com

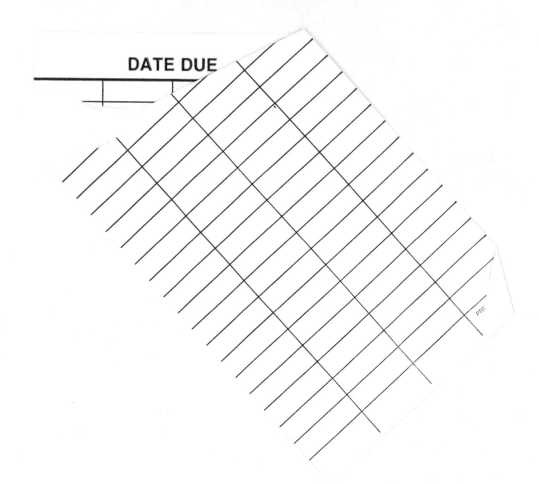

DATE DUE